The God Beyond Your Wildest Dreams

A Study Guide

The God Beyond Your Wildest Dreams

A Study Guide

James Berglund

Pacific Press®
Publishing Association
Nampa, Idaho | Oshawa, Ontario, Canada
www.pacificpress.com

Cover design by Steve Lanto
Cover design resources from iStockphoto.com/480890344
Inside design by Bryan Gray

The author assumes full responsibility for the accuracy of all facts and quotations as cited in this book.

You can obtain additional copies of this book by calling toll-free 1-800-765-6955 or by visiting http://www.adventistbookcenter.com.

Unless otherwise indicated, all Scripture quotations are taken from the NEW AMERICAN STANDARD BIBLE®, copyright © 1960, 1962, 1963, 1968, 1971, 1972, 1973, 1975, 1977, 1995 by the Lockman Foundation. Used by permission.

Scripture quotations marked ESV are from the Holy Bible, English Standard Version®, (ESV®), copyright © 2001 by Crossway, a publishing ministry of Good News Publishers. Used by permission. All rights reserved.

Scripture quotations marked GNT are from the Good News Translation® (Today's English Version, Second Edition). Copyright © 1992 American Bible Society. All rights reserved.

Scripture quotations marked GW are taken from GOD'S WORD, a copyrighted work of God's Word to the Nations. Quotations are used by permission. Copyright © 1995 by God's Word to the Nations. All rights reserved.

Scripture quotations marked ISV are taken from *The Holy Bible: International Standard Version*. Copyright © 1995–2014 by ISV Foundation. All rights reserved internationally. Used by permission of Davidson Press, LLC.

Scripture quotations marked KJV are from the King James Version.

Scripture quotations taken from *The Message*. Copyright © 1993, 1994, 1995, 1996, 2000, 2001, 2002. Used by permission of NavPress Publishing Group.

Scripture quotations marked NEB are from the *New English Bible*, copyright © Cambridge University Press and Oxford University Press 1961, 1970. All rights reserved.

Scripture quotations marked NIV® are taken from the THE HOLY BIBLE, NEW INTERNATIONAL VERSION®. Copyright © 1973, 1978, 1984, 2011 by Biblica, Inc.® Used by permission. All rights reserved worldwide.

Scripture quotations marked NKJV are from the New King James Version®. Copyright © 1982 by Thomas Nelson. Used by permission. All rights reserved.

Scripture quotations marked NLT are taken from the Holy Bible, New Living Translation, copyright © 1996, 2004, 2007, 2013, 2015 by Tyndale House Foundation. Used by permission of Tyndale House Publishers, Inc., Carol Stream, Illinois 60188. All rights reserved.

Scriptures quotations marked RSV are from the Revised Standard Version of the Bible, copyright © 1946, 1952, 1971 by the Division of Christian Education of the National Council of the Churches of Christ in the U.S.A. Used by permission.

Scripture quotations marked YLT are from Young's Literal Translation.

Library of Congress Cataloging-in-Publication Data
Names: Berglund, James, 1959– author.
Title: The God beyond your wildest dreams : a study guide / Jim Berglund.
Description: Nampa : Pacific Press Publishing, 2017.
Identifiers: LCCN 2016055177 | ISBN 9780816362547 (pbk.)
Subjects: LCSH: God (Christianity) | Theology, Doctrinal—Popular works. |
   General Conference of Seventh-day Adventists—Doctrines.
Classification: LCC BT103 .B469 2017 | DDC 231.7—dc23 LC record available at https://lccn.loc.gov/2016055177

February 2017

Dedication

I dedicate this book to those who cheered me on to write and rewrite this volume.

To my son-in-law David Bonjour

You purposely sacrifice to make my daughter happy. You demonstrate servant leadership in giving yourself for team ministry. You continue to do the right thing even when it is hard. God has gifted you.

To my son, Pastor Joshua Hester

I love who you are: passionate for Jesus, a deep thinker, honesty transparent, and genuinely fun. Thanks for being my accountability partner, and, among men, my best friend.

To my angel girl, JaLynn Berglund

Jesus' heart lives in you to care for the battered, bruised, and broken. You love with compassion, gentleness, and kindness, and are fiercely loyal. God has gifted you as a poet and writer.

To my princess, Pastor Shelina Bonjour

You bring joy, life, laughter, and energy wherever you go. You remain a light in my life. To see you live out Jesus' call to ministry brings me joy. God works through you to draw others to Him.

To my love, Shelly Berglund

You are the heart of our family. Thanks for being my lifelong partner in ministry, my all-time best friend and companion, my greatest cheerleader, and the one who pastors me as the pastor. Thank you for the hours of family time you sacrificed to allow me time to write this book.

Contents

9   Introduction

13   Chapter 1: The God Who Pursues Me

21   Chapter 2: The God Behind the Scenes

29   Chapter 3: The God Who Came to Earth

37   Chapter 4: The Warrior Coach

45   Chapter 5: Spiritual Fusion

53   Chapter 6: The Family Mission Statement

59   Chapter 7: The Creator's Gift to Me

67   Chapter 8: Family as It Was Meant to Be

73   Chapter 9: Principles to Live By

79   Chapter 10: God Makes Me Whole

87   Chapter 11: Security as His Managers

93   Chapter 12: The Profit of a Prophet

99   Chapter 13: The King Is Coming

103   Chapter 14: The Fountain of Life

109   Chapter 15: The Custody Battle

117   Chapter 16: Finally Home

Let Me Introduce You to the God Beyond Your Wildest Dreams

Wait right there, Pastor." Margie put her hand up in the universal "stop" sign. She interrupted me in my first attempt to introduce her to Jesus: "I've heard that salvation stuff before. But it's for good girls, innocent girls, not the likes of me. I've been around." With one hand, she gestured, drawing attention to the tattoos on her arms. "I've done things that would make a sailor blush. My heart's as black as that there cup of coffee.

"As a little girl I went to church, then drifted away and messed up. A lot of water has passed under the bridge since then. He has enough on me now to permanently bar me from the pearly gates, let alone steppin' through your church doors. You're delivering your message to the wrong address trying to rescue me. I'm beyond saving. I assure you He doesn't want me."

"Margie, I promise you that He wants you! From the day you walked away from His church and from His heart, He has pursued you like a lost treasure. Like an anxious mother staying up until her daughter returns home from her date, He eagerly awaits your return. With each sunrise, He reminds you that He renews His mercy every day. He assures you that His arms of forgiveness long to embrace you. Each expression of love for you, from your sister's gifts to the unexpected hug of a neighbor's child, originates in His heart. He whispers your name in the night's cool breeze. He still counts you as His daughter. He replays in your memory the songs of praise you sang to Him as a child, keeping you connected to Him, reminding you not just that He loves you but that you love Him too. He sacrificed Himself to get you back, because His family will not be complete without you. Margie, I tell you again, He loves you!"

She stared at me glassy-eyed and said nothing for a moment, then, choking back the tears, she said, "That's the God I wish I knew. If He were like you just said, then even I would have hope. But the God you just described is a God beyond my wildest dreams."

I broke into a smile. "Then let me introduce you to the God beyond your wildest dreams."

John

"Pastor, I feel spiritually blah. I've grown up with 'the truth.' I have been a Seventh-day Adventist all my life. I have kept the right day of worship but seldom had an encounter with God on that day. I have effectively argued points of theology with other Christians, using proof texts to back up my viewpoint while at the same time wondering, if they accepted my truth, could they maintain the vibrant relationship they currently had with God? I have paid my tithes and offerings but would refer to myself as a 'dutiful giver' rather than a 'cheerful giver.'

"I have heard that I am part of the remnant, and I have the judgment hour message to preach to the world, but it brings me so much fear and insecurity that I certainly don't want to lay this burden on someone else. I am a thoroughbred Seventh-day Adventist. I would never think of eating pork, but tradition dictates my choice, not my relationship to God. Some of the other lifestyle specifics I see as my parents' applications to religion, not as mine. I believe we go to the grave when we die rather than heaven or hell, but it seems like spiritual trivia with no real significance to real life. I feel spiritually lethargic. I need a spiritual energy boost. Can you help me?"

"John, you need a deeper picture of God. Let me introduce you to the God beyond your wildest dreams."

Knowing God better

What we believe about God's character affects our relationship with Him. Separately, conservatives and liberals present a partial picture of God and distort His character. On the conservative side, this results in people serving a tyrannical God whose chief attribute is stern justice. With fearful obedience, they tremble before Him, working fervently to measure up to an unobtainable standard. On the liberal side, this results in people claiming Christianity yet living in unbridled sin, excusing their behavior by confessing themselves as "only human." They view God as a doting grandfather, who, in the end, will mercifully overlook their transgressions and save them anyway. They miss the love that motivates them to live righteously. They have not drawn close enough to God to let His presence transform them. They readily ignore the things they once believed, never comprehending the beautiful principles behind them. They want Him to give them salvation but not live in them.

Both sides endorse half-truths, finding scriptural support for their viewpoint. They don't analyze all of Scripture and discover that *they* fall short of the whole truth. Witnesses in our court of law must pledge "to tell the truth, *the whole truth*, and nothing but the truth." A half-truth constitutes a lie. For those who need a vision of God in His fullness, let me introduce you to the God beyond your wildest dreams.

Have you been through pain that caused you to question God and His love for you? Has your contact with Christians turned you away from God? What if the things you believed about Him that caused you to reject Him were lies? What if He passionately loves you and craves your presence? What if the God beyond your wildest dreams really exists?

Maybe you haven't left Him but still dream of a different sort of God. What if the God you have dedicated your life to has abilities that far exceed your imagination? Have you settled for a Clark Kent God because you refuse to allow Him to act as the beyond-Superman God He really is? What if He has enough power to give you victory in your spiritual life? What if popular opinion about God, even Christian popular opinion, is wrong? What if a personal God lives behind the rules you have followed? Then the potential for discovering the God beyond your wildest dreams might rest in these pages as they unveil Scripture's revelation of God's true character. Let me introduce you to the God beyond your wildest dreams.

Thoughts to Ponder

1. In what ways am I like Margie? In what ways am I like John?

_____

_____

_____

2. Did I once have a closer connection to Jesus? What changed that? What am I waiting for to restore the relationship?

_____

_____

_____

3. In my heart, have I been apathetic toward God because I honestly wasn't sure I liked all that I knew about God? Where have I received the bulk of my information about God? Was it from a person or from my own study?

_____

_____

_____

4. Am I willing to investigate new concepts of God? If I have questions, will I follow through on the scriptural references given?

_____

_____

_____

5. Prayer: God, please use this study time to show me more about You. Help me to move deeper using a factual understanding about You to create a deeper relationship with You. Please meet me here in this search for a deeper connection with You.

_____

_____

_____

CHAPTER 1

The God Who Pursues Me

P arty hearty,' I said to myself each night. But I woke up in the morning feeling empty. Drugs, alcohol, fancy foods, and fine women never gratified my cravings. Finding no lasting contentment, I launched public works programs and organized cultural experiences in the arts. While others may have been enriched, I felt like a dog chasing his tail. I sought a remedy for a life sick with meaninglessness.

"I threw myself into my career, obtaining fame, power, money, and treasures. I had it all, things of which others only dream. Yet I found myself grasping at soap bubbles. All the iridescent promises of these pursuits burst as I held them. I spent my life chasing the wind" (Ecclesiastes 2:1–11, author's paraphrase).

King Solomon's experience parallels our search for meaning and contentment in life. We grasp for the beauty of the soap bubbles' iridescent promises, then *pop!* they burst and leave us empty. Some relentlessly travel the roads Solomon described, chasing one soap bubble after the next, but they never reach their sought-after destination. They spend their lives pursuing what they will never obtain. Others become disillusioned and give up, convinced that true contentment, like Aesop's sour grapes, remains unattainable. They settle for half-lives, rummaging through the garbage cans for life's scraps.

God gives us hope. In Him, we find love, meaning, purpose, and satisfaction. When restored to our Creator, we become whole again. The gospel explains how God restores mankind after sin.

A voting booth in Eden
Adam and Eve's hearts beat as one with God, completely united with Him in purity and righteousness. Like trusting children, they freely rested in the love and provision of their heavenly Father. Wanting beings that loved Him, and not robots programed to mimic responses of love, the Father created His children with the choice to love Him or leave Him.

God placed two trees as a voting booth in Eden to demonstrate their choice for or against His governing their lives (Genesis 2:9). As Adam and Eve ate from the tree of life, they demonstrated their allegiance to God, the source of life. God, like a nurturing Father, explained that rejecting His rule by choosing the tree of the knowledge of good and evil meant death because they would separate themselves from the only source of life (Genesis 2:16, 17). God warned them of the rebellious angelic prince who had a vendetta to settle against Him because He cast him out of heaven.

The adversary introduced distrust in his attempt to separate Adam and Eve from a life of

This chapter is based on Seventh-day Adventist fundamental beliefs no. 3, "The Father"; no. 9, "The Life, Death, and Resurrection of Christ"; and no. 10, "The Experience of Salvation."

blissful contentment with Yahweh, their personal God. Satan came disguised as an ancient serpent—then one of God's most beautiful creatures (Jewish tradition pictures the serpent as a golden dragon; when stretched out, his translucent wings were formed with multicolored, scalelike feathers that glistened in the sunlight like transparent rainbows).

"He spoke to the Woman: 'Do I understand that God told you not to eat from any tree in the garden?' " (Genesis 3:1, *The Message*). As a master manipulator, Satan lured Eve into a conversation. She defended God: "Not at all. We can eat from the trees in the garden. It's only about the tree in the middle of the garden that God said, 'Don't eat from it; don't even touch it or you'll die' " (Genesis 3:2, 3, *The Message*). "The serpent told the Woman, 'You won't die' " (Genesis 3:4, *The Message*). In other words, "You don't need God for life."

Satan indirectly accused God of lying. The tempter knew that he could not rip Adam and Eve from God's protection; they must choose him over God (Genesis 3:5). He vilified God as jealously suppressing their potential because He feared they would become His equal. Satan masks himself as their "savior," empowering them to become the "gods" they were destined to be.

Sin's allurement

If sin did not have a promised reward, we would never choose it. Satan baits the hook, promising exhilarating happiness, an exalted position, or a new state of freedom. He lies—his native language—like the stereotypical used-car salesman, saying whatever will get us to buy the product. Sin never delivers what it promises; even its pleasure lasts only a short season (Hebrews 11:25).

Satan gives away the first hit of sin like a corner drug pusher giving out free samples, never intimating the addiction that allows him, as their dealer, to own them. They will give up their morals, lose their dreams, betray their loved ones, and literally sell their souls for this quick fix. So often we fall for the same lines. He gives the lure of the drinking party but doesn't allude to hugging the toilet the next morning. He promises physical pleasure for the playboy lifestyle but doesn't reference the empty loneliness of sex without committed love, the devastating diagnosis of HIV, or the possibility of an unwanted pregnancy. He lures us with material wealth but doesn't disclose the empty lives of those who have already reached the top.

Sin has a hook, not just the death at the end of our lives but lives riddled with pain. Satan misrepresented God to Adam and Eve as withholding the good life. He denied the painful consequences of acting against God. He promised special pleasure from sin. Even with all that humanity has been through, we still buy into the lie that sin will not harm us.

I have always dreamed of flying—really flying—unaided by some mechanical device. Standing on top of a sixty-four-story building, the urge comes over me to jump and experience the exhilaration of flying through the air. Knowing the consequential *splat* that waits at the bottom prevents me from jumping. Those few seconds of pleasure don't outweigh the consequences of the indulgence. The recognition of more pain than gain disarms the power of the temptation.

Distrust: The core of sin

Distrust in God constitutes the core issue of sin. We commit adultery because we don't believe God that fidelity to our spouse will ultimately bring our greatest happiness. We steal because we don't believe that God will provide for us. We worship other gods because we don't trust Yahweh to be God enough to handle our lives. We covet what our neighbor has, not trusting that God has *our* best in mind. All sin comes because we distrust God.

When Adam and Eve did not exercise faith or trust in God, they sinned. "Whatever does not proceed from faith is sin" (Romans 14:23, ESV). They relied on their own wisdom, informed by Satan. "When the woman saw that the tree was good for food, and that it was a delight to the eyes, and that the tree was desirable to make one wise, she took from its fruit and ate; and she gave also to her husband with her, and he ate" (Genesis 3:6).

The serpent beguiles Eve, but Adam makes his choice with full knowledge of his actions. What thought process would allow him to betray his God? Realizing Eve had rejected God, did he fear that God might destroy her, leaving him alone? Did he put her before God? The real issue was that he didn't trust that God was big enough to work things out for his good.

Why didn't he talk to God about his problem first? If he had trusted God, what might have been the results? Would God still have died for Eve and given her life? Then would He have returned her to faithful Adam to nurture as his wife? Would Adam have remained the head of an unfallen race? Or would God have created a new wife for Adam? Our answers would amount to speculation. The point remains that even after Eve sinned, Adam could have trusted God and remained faithful, but instead he fell for Satan's trap.

Thinking they would rule their own lives as gods, they took the throne. They not only sinned, they became sinful by nature. They lived with the three S's on the throne: Satan, Sin, and Self.

LOW GAME: The result of a broken relationship

I will illustrate the result of a broken relationship with God with the acronym LOW GAME:

- They experienced *Loneliness*: they missed God as their companion.
- They were *Outcasts*: they could not remain in God's presence.
- They felt *Worthless*: their value had been in their connection with God.
- They knew *Guilt*: they had disobeyed God.
- They felt deep *Anxiety*: God no longer protected them.
- They knew *Meaninglessness*: their purpose had been to commune with and serve God.
- They felt *Empty*: no matter what else we use to try to fill it, a spot remains empty that only God can fill.

The results of the loss of a love connection with God caused mankind to seek for love outside of God's will. A sinful nature resulting from a broken connection with God produced sins. "Sin is the transgression of the law" (1 John 3:4, KJV). Sinful actions come from a sinful nature just as sure as lemons come from a lemon tree.

Missing God—the source of love—we desperately spin out of control. People search for love through adultery, fornication, pedophilia, and homosexuality. Gangs gather kids who want to belong and be loved. Some give up on love and act out in hate. Others turn to drinking and drugs to escape the guilt of living apart from God. Some seek to make themselves more loveable by obtaining things or position.

The corporate head

Adam and Eve's sin affected all mankind. "Therefore, just as through one man sin entered into the world, and death through sin, and so death spread to all men, because all sinned" (Romans 5:12). "For as through the one man's disobedience the many were made sinners" (Romans 5:19).

Adam filled the role of mankind's corporate representative. When he chose to separate himself from God by disobedience, he placed the entire race under bondage to Satan. The Western world's strong emphasis on individuality makes understanding corporate representation difficult. Middle Eastern culture stresses interdependence. One person's action reflects on the whole community. The choices of the head of the family affect his entire progeny. In our country, if the president decides to go into war, the nation is at war whether or not we individually agree with his choice.

Because of our heredity and this law of corporate representation, at birth we receive a selfish nature, one under Satan's rule. Before the American Civil War, people born into slavery became the property of their parents' master. The master didn't need to purchase them; they were automatically his slaves. Similarly, because of the choice made by Adam and Eve, we were born enslaved to Satan.

We are "by nature children of wrath, even as the rest" (Ephesians 2:3). Not just our actions fall under God's wrath but our very being. David admitted this, saying, "I was brought forth in iniquity, and in sin my mother conceived me" (Psalm 51:5). In our selfish nature, we turn to our own way (Isaiah 53:6), and we perform sinful acts.

Can we choose to be good?

So can we just choose to act contrary to our nature? Can we muster up willpower and become better men and women? "Can the Ethiopian change his skin or the leopard his spots? Then you also can do good who are accustomed to doing evil" (Jeremiah 13:23).

God answers a resounding No! Even the best we have to offer on our own power will be less than nothing. "For all of us have become like one who is unclean, and all our righteous deeds are like a filthy garment; and all of us wither like a leaf, and our iniquities, like the wind, take us away" (Isaiah 64:6). The full meaning of this text hit me when a professor shared with me that the Hebrew word for "filthy rag" refers specifically to a menstrual rag—bloody, disgusting, and foul.

Imagine a disappointed lemon tree trying to become an apple tree by cutting off its sour lemons and hanging sweet apples in their place. The apples will rot off and more lemons will grow back. Try as it might, the lemon tree can only produce those sour little fruits. In the same way, the end consequence of our nature is death (Romans 6:23). Sin reigns in our natural body (Romans 6:12).

God wants us back

God desires *everyone* to be saved. He does not wish "for any to perish but for all to come to repentance" (2 Peter 3:9; see also 1 Timothy 2:3, 4). From the beginning, He has not withheld anything that was for our good, but He has been misrepresented as desiring to destroy us.

Instead, as Moses found out, the Lord God is "compassionate and gracious, slow to anger, and abounding in lovingkindness and truth; who keeps lovingkindness for thousands, who forgives iniquity, transgression and sin; yet He will by no means leave the guilty unpunished, visiting the iniquity of fathers on the children and on the grandchildren to the third and fourth generations" (Exodus 34:6, 7). Sin creates a separation between us and God (Isaiah 59:2).

How can a holy, righteous, and pure God also love, forgive, and care for sinners? Our compassionate Lord found a way to meet the challenge of maintaining both mercy and justice. He could not ignore the choice Adam and Eve had made.

Satan thought he had God: if God chose to let Adam and Eve go free, He would defy His own law. Satan's charge that God's law was arbitrary would be substantiated. Then Satan, too, would have to be allowed access to heaven. Or if God decided to act in justice, He would have to destroy His own children. This would be a devastating blow to a God of love.

But God had an answer that would allow Him to be both merciful and just. He could not ignore Adam and Eve's choice of Satan, sin, and death. But He provided them with another choice. They could accept the Son of God's death in their place. "For God so loved the world, that he gave his only begotten Son, that whoever believeth in him should not perish, but have everlasting life" (John 3:16, KJV). How would this work?

A second Adam

God would create a second Adam in Jesus, another corporate head of mankind (Romans 5:14). He was born connected with God through the Holy Spirit (Luke 1:35; Matthew 1:20). His purpose as Adam II was to restore what the first Adam's fall had lost.

Jesus came to free us from the slavery of Satan so that we too might live in freedom from sin (Romans 8:12, 13). "Therefore, since the children share in flesh and blood, He Himself likewise also partook of the same, that through death He might render powerless him who had the power of death, that is, the devil, and might free those who through fear of death were subject to slavery all their lives" (Hebrews 2:14, 15). God planned not just to pay a price for sin but to free us from Satan's captivity. First John 3:4 says, "Sin is lawlessness." Jesus came "to take away sins" and "destroy the works of the devil" (1 John 3:5, 8). How would Jesus deal with man's captivity to Satan? He would ransom us, just as today someone might ransom a child from a kidnapper.

Jesus was led by the Spirit into the wilderness to be tempted on the same grounds that the first Adam fell (Matthew 4:1–10). In each temptation, Satan tempted Jesus to distrust His heavenly Father. He wanted Jesus to use His divine powers to meet His own need, instead of relying on the Father's plan, timing, and power (Romans 5:19). Jesus came through as a conqueror. Adam II trusts God.

Satan had no claim on Jesus' life. "The ruler of the world is coming, and he has nothing in Me" (John 14:30). Clearly, God reigned on the throne of Jesus' life.

The choice to stay connected to God resulted in the only victorious, sinless human life. The fruit of the Spirit was perfectly reflected in His life (Galatians 5:22, 23). Just as a lemon tree produces lemons, an apple tree produces apples. Jesus chose to stay connected with the Father and produced the apple fruit of righteousness.

Such a life connected with God the Father results in eternal life. Christ's life was an example of victory. As the corporate head for all mankind, He lived righteously.

The great exchange

The problem remains—you and I are born with the first Adam's nature, not the Second Adam's. How can we gain access to His eternal life?

God provided a way. He moved in like a hostage negotiator in a kidnapping. Jesus made freeing us His first priority. God ransoms us "from the futile ways inherited from your forefathers, not with perishable things such as silver or gold, but with the precious blood of Christ, like that of a lamb without blemish or spot" (1 Peter 1:18, 19, ESV). Jesus stepped in and exchanged His life that we might go free. Some translations use the term *redeemed* instead of *ransomed*. We redeem a coupon by exchanging it for the purchased item. Jesus exchanged His righteous human life for ours. He gave us a new choice, the choice to accept His death for ours.

Jesus our Savior saves us *from* our sin, not *in* our sin. He frees us from having Satan, sin, and self in the control seat of our lives and allows us to place God in the control seat of our lives.

The cross forms the bridge that connects us to the perfect life of Jesus Christ, the Second Adam and our Savior. The cross makes the great exchange possible. "He made Him who knew no sin to be sin on our behalf, so that we might become the righteousness of God in Him" (2 Corinthians 5:21).

Jesus as Savior and Lord

Jesus' sacrifice on the cross does not just free us from sin's penalty. Adam II becomes our family head, placing God on the control seat of our lives. We cannot accept Jesus' work as Savior without also accepting Him as Lord.

Accepting His work of justification and sanctification means not only accepting what Jesus has done for us but also what He does in us. Much of Christendom accepts Jesus as Savior, accepting what He did in laying down His life for them, without accepting Him as Lord and allowing Him to rule. They live believing Jesus gives them eternal life ultimately but that practically Satan still controls their lives.

The process of moving from a life with Satan in control to a life with Jesus in control we call being *born again*. The very term reveals our first birth as inadequate (John 3:3). The rebirth concept made complete sense to the Jews offering salvation to Gentiles. Proselytes entered the Jewish faith through baptism symbolizing their rebirth as a Jew.

Jesus tells Nicodemus that he must be born again. He wanted him to know that a heart rebirth was necessary in order to belong to God—meaning Jesus must reign in the heart.

God also described the process of conversion as when He removes the heart of stone and gives a heart of flesh (Ezekiel 36:26). The change from a nature where Satan, sin, and self are on the throne to God being in the control seat of the life is also referred to as becoming a *new creature* or *creation*. "Therefore if anyone is in Christ, he is a new creature; the old things passed away; behold, new things have come" (2 Corinthians 5:17)! We have a new Master. The love of God controls us instead of the selfish desires of the flesh (2 Corinthians 5:14).

The fruit of God on the throne

Fruit naturally comes from connecting with Jesus like branches connect to the vine (John 15). Apart from Jesus we can do nothing. The change of the heart from a lemon tree to an apple tree produces apples, not lemons.

When a king comes and takes over the land of a hostile dictator, the land takes a while to reflect the king's rule and for it to filter into every aspect of life. God places the former dictator behind bars and takes away his power (Romans 6:6). Young's Literal Translation of this verse says, "Knowing, that our old man was crucified with [him], that the body of the sin may be made useless, for our no longer serving the sin." The International Standard Version says, "We know that our old natures were crucified with him so that our sin-laden bodies might be rendered powerless and we might no longer be slaves to sin."

Our old nature resists being locked up, so Satan, drawing on the old man within us, takes his little metal cup and runs it against the bars, doing what I call the "jailhouse rock" of temptation. He reminds us of the pleasures of sin—baiting the hook. We decide whether we will trust him or trust Jesus. If we resist, he flees, growing weaker, and his influence on us becomes less and less (James 4:7). The nature that we feed, and allow to exercise in our life, grows strongest.

Saving faith

Our part in salvation goes beyond a belief that consists of intellectual consent—even demons believe (James 2:19). With saving faith, I surrender my life to God's reign. In order to trust people, I have to first believe that they *care* about me and have my good in mind. Second, I must know they *can* accomplish the work necessary for my good.

In order for me to trust God I have to know that He both wants the best for my life and He is able to make that best happen! I build that trust the same way I build trust in my human relationships. I watch how He treats others. I look for His character traits and their consistency.

I learn from the Bible and Christians' testimonies how God treats people. The psalmist states, "No good thing does He withhold from those who walk uprightly" (Psalm 84:11). Little by little I turn over the things in my life, and I watch how God handles them. And when I find Him to be absolutely trustworthy, I give Him not just parts of my life but my life itself. And after knowing Him for these many years I find Him—the God beyond my wildest dreams.

Thoughts to Ponder

1. How does this description of salvation differ from others that I have heard?

_____

_____

_____

2. What sort of tree does my "fruit" indicate? Have I tried to tie on fruit instead of having my tree trunk changed?

_____

_____

_____

3. Have I judged the sin of others as worse than my own? Can I see others through a new light, realizing sins are an individual's search for the lost love of God inside?

_____

_____

_____

4. Does viewing salvation from this perspective give me a different view of the character of God? How do I understand righteousness by faith?

_____

_____

_____

5. In what actions do I invite the old man back on the throne of my heart? Have I accepted Jesus as both Lord and Savior?

_____

_____

_____

CHAPTER 2

The God Behind the Scenes

I see him in my mind's eye, handing an envelope bulging with cash to a stooped-over widow who finds herself short on this month's mortgage payment. She stands at the door and receives the gift. She takes his hand in hers and chokes out a gentle "Thank you" as she gazes into his eyes with tears of gratitude. On his way home from work, he stops to buy something to drink from the kids at their lemonade stand. They try to act so grown up and businesslike as he slips a large tip into the young entrepreneurs' cup, but their giggles betray their childish glee.

He habitually took time from his busy schedule to care for others' needs. He set up and helped maintain a house for battered women, and he personally sponsored five addicted teens through drug rehab. He regularly sent scriptural notes of inspiration to his sons or whispered advice to them to bring home flowers for their wives. He knelt together with his wife and prayed a hedge of protection around their family.

While these specifics come from my imagination, Scripture makes it clear that Job lived an exemplary life before God. He consistently encouraged his kids to commit their lives to God, and he offered sacrifices just in case any of them sinned (Job 1:4–6). He hated evil and loved righteousness so much that God identifies him as blameless in His sight (Job 1:1). Not only were Job's outside actions visible to all who looked on, but God's own testimony of blessing rested upon him. God blessed him with three daughters and seven sons.

God multiplied tokens of His approval on Job: seven thousand sheep, three thousand camels, one thousand oxen, and five hundred donkeys. Various servants and field hands rounded out Job's wealth. In the eyes of the people, all of this confirmed that God Himself had judged that Job was worthy of His blessing. The people would naturally equate Job being the richest man with Job being the most righteous man. Job's blessing also reflected on both God's ability and His desire to reward those who served Him. Just as God used His blessing on Israel to attract people to serve Him, so His blessing on Job served to reinforce how God desired to shower blessings on those who would completely yield their lives to Him. The whole community could point to this astounding man, challenging each other and their children to live righteously. Maybe the adage "You reap what you sow" started here (see also Galatians 6:7). Job served as the poster child for how God rewards the faithful.

Then, in a single day, Job's world came crashing down as messengers, one after another, brought devastating news. The first arrived and breathlessly reported that unprovoked Sabeans attacked them, killed Job's servants in cold blood, and stole his cattle and donkeys. This servant had barely finished speaking when another servant stumbled through the

This chapter is based on Seventh-day Adventist fundamental belief no. 8, "The Great Controversy."

doors, bringing a tale of a supernatural thunderstorm. Fireballs of lightning rolled along the ground and killed both sheep and shepherds until all were wiped out except the messenger himself.

When the next servant stumbled into Job's presence, he brought a sense of foreboding. The Chaldeans' raiding party had attacked, killed his servants, and taken his camels. While Job was reeling with the horrible news, a final servant came bearing a grievous tale: in the midst of a family celebration, a hurricane-force wind hit the house with such devastating effect that the house collapsed, killing all his family (Job 1:13–19). Only Job and his wife survive.

From the community's perspective, something had changed. The circumstances indicated that Job no longer enjoyed God's blessing, but why? Had God ceased to be the sovereign God? Was it that He could bless Job but lacked power enough to protect him? Had God ceased being a good God? Was He in a mood swing that caused Him to involuntarily lash out? Not being willing to believe any of these about God, they could only come to one conclusion: Job's sin made him an enemy of God.

Even though the circumstances produced some self-doubting, Job knew that he had been faithful to God. So what did he think? Job's response reveals his experience with God and challenges me to find a faith experience as deep as his. "He said, 'Naked I came from my mother's womb, and naked I shall return there. The LORD gave and the LORD has taken away. Blessed be the name of the LORD' " (Job 1:21). Job continued holding onto God even when a second attack hits him physically, giving him painful boils that made him wish he had never been born. Don't misunderstand; Job wrestled with God, but at the same time he clung to God. Though he didn't understand God's action, he yielded to God's sovereignty and praised His name.

Suffering can damage our picture of God

Not many of us go through pain, suffering, and loss like Job and come out on the other end still with a positive picture of God. Oftentimes, because we don't have the experience with God ourselves, or because our community doesn't believe in God, we call God's goodness or sovereignty into question. In our scientific age, we evaluate based on the facts before us. But God in the book of Job pulls the curtains back so that we can see what has been done surreptitiously. He gives us perspective beyond this world's dimension. He lets us see behind the scenes.

Perspective makes all the difference, such as the day when Eugene cried from the back seat of the car, "Mom, Jason is hitting me!" Mom turns and witnesses Jason hitting his brother multiple times on the shoulder. She screams for him to stop and pulls over and yanks Jason out of the car. As he attempts to explain that Eugene provoked him, she gives the five-year-old a spanking. She saw him hit his brother with her own two eyes!

Jason doesn't talk the rest of the trip. Mom has judged unfairly; she didn't see Eugene behind the scenes, poking, prodding, pinching, and punching him. Jason tried ignoring his brat of a brother, tried moving farther away toward the window, and tried telling him to stop, but to no avail. Finally, he reached his boiling point. Eugene plays the role of the victim when really he was the instigator. If only Mom's eyes in the back of her head had allowed her to see behind the scenes.

Just as Mom wrongly judged Jason, missing what happened behind the scenes, we can misjudge God. We witness what we believe is a reprehensible act on God's part, but we don't have His perspective.

Imagine sitting in a restaurant when, behind you at a table across from yours, a commotion arises. All the patrons direct their attention toward that table. When you look, a chair lies tipped back and the dinner guest lies on the floor with a man hovering over him. You witness him take a steak knife from the table and plunge it into the victim's throat. A woman at the table beside yours screams, and utter chaos breaks out in the restaurant as people panic and run. What do you feel toward the man with the knife? Would you consider hiring him, or allow him to date your daughter, or bring him to your home for dinner?

Now, what if I told you that he was an emergency room doctor, and he had plunged the knife in his friend's throat as a calculated emergency medical procedure to save his best friend's life? With this new perspective, instead of labeling him a villain, you pronounce him a hero. Instead of wanting jail time for him, you want an award banquet in his name. You would be proud to make his acquaintance.

Once you have this additional information and a broader understanding, your whole feeling about the man's character changes. The act of his stabbing a knife into another living human being has not changed. Your feelings toward the doctor adjust as you understand the whole picture. Maybe with the behind-the-scenes look provided in the book of Job, we will come up with a fuller understanding of God and the problem of pain.

God reveals what goes on behind the scenes

God reveals a heavenly meeting that prompted Job's day of destruction. One day the sons of God gathered in heaven before God (Job 1:6). I could speculate that this meeting hosted the ruling representatives of the inhabited planets of the universe, but Scripture doesn't give these specifics. It only tells us that Satan appeared with the sons of God. God questions, "From where do you come?" (Job 1:7). God seems to be asking, "What planet do you claim to represent? By what authority do you come to this gathering of the hosts of the universe?" Satan answers, "From roaming about on the earth and walking around on it" (Job 1:7).

God's response seems unexpected. "Have you considered My servant Job?" (Job 1:8). In other words, "Satan, you claim that you represent the earth, but the earth still belongs to Me. Job still serves Me. I still have faithful loyal followers." So God pointed to Job and said, "He lives faithfully to Me as My exhibit A. I still claim earth because I have a man who has enthroned Me as his God."

Paraphrasing Satan's counter: "Does Job serve You out of love and reverence? I think not. He serves You because of what he gets from You. He views You as nothing more than a heavenly sugar daddy. It's not You whom he loves; it's the riches that he loves. So if You took those things away from him he would curse You to Your face" (see Job 1:9–11).

A cosmic struggle: The great controversy

Job's story reveals God and Satan locked behind the scenes in a battle for mankind. We catch a glimpse of the nature and character of the two powers. Satan tempts God to strike Job's family and wealth. *God refuses!* God's nature will not allow Him to do that. The same thing happens later when Job records an almost identical scene, only this time Satan tempts God to strike Job's person. Again *God refuses*. He allows Satan access to Job's person. In this experiment, Job reveals the contrast of God's nature of love, loyalty, and compassion with Satan's nature of destruction, hatred, and wickedness.

It amazes me that the entire Old Testament contains only three passages that mention Satan by name. Understanding the polytheistic culture of that time, it surprises me that God would mention Satan at all. He risked the people perceiving Satan as an evil god for them to appease. God carefully led them to understand that He alone possesses divinity. He declares through Moses, "Hear, O Israel! The LORD is our God, the LORD is one!" (Deuteronomy 6:4). And yet He so desires for His people to understand His heart that He purposefully exposes Satan, whose name literally means "the Adversary." Through the use of story and symbol, and this key passage in Job, God opens the picture of the circumstances behind the scenes.

Jesus came to earth to enlighten mankind concerning God's true character. He also exposed Satan's nature and his role as a propaganda artist.

False-flag terrorism

In this controversy, Satan has engaged for centuries in false-flag terrorism, which occurs when a government stages an attack on its own people. The instigators blame others in an attempt to sway public opinion toward themselves, to label another group as an enemy, to justify going to war, to cover their own actions, or to stimulate the approval of a total break with, or annihilation of, the enemy. This concept gains its name from the practice of ships flying the flags or colors of the enemy and attacking friends in order to create allies against their enemies.

Satan has been engaged in false-flag terrorism since the beginning. He continually lashes out to cause pain and suffering to humanity, and then he blames God. Lying comes so naturally to Satan that Jesus calls it his mother tongue (John 8:44). Satan tells us what we want to hear. He paints a picture of a leisurely life with him, and then, once we fall for his promo and he has us signed on the dotted line, we start recognizing all the things we missed in the fine print that make our life a living hell. Thankfully, Jesus pulled off the devil's disguise and exposed his true colors. Just as Satan caused Job's pain, Jesus points to the devil as the source of all pain.

Jesus compares the kingdom of heaven to a man sowing seed in a field. When the garden starts growing, weeds grow beside the beautiful plants. The master's servants question him. "Master, did you not sow good seed in your field? How then does it have weeds?" (Matthew 13:27, ESV). "He said to them, 'An enemy has done this' " (Matthew 13:28 ESV). Jesus decodes His parable for the disciples: "The weeds are the sons of the evil one, and the enemy who sowed them is the devil" (Matthew 13:38, 39, ESV). Jesus makes it clear that Satan, not God, planted the evil seed that sprouts evil and causes physical suffering and pain. When a woman seeks Him for healing, Jesus announces that Satan bound her for eighteen long years (Luke 13:16).

I think of how often I have heard people doing exactly what Job's friends did—declaring that the pain in life comes from God. In order to explain the agony, they declare they know

God's purpose for the suffering. With their limited view of the great controversy, they analyze the situation and announce that God must be punishing wickedness, refining or strengthening character, or tearing someone down in order to gain glory for Himself when He builds us up.

Satan's role in suffering

The great controversy opens an additional explanation. God allows Satan to act in order to reveal Satan's true character, letting the universe see the results of a world under the hand of the fallen angel. Could the rebel have brought assertions against God's character that can only be answered by God allowing the world to observe Satan's character? What if Satan claimed that God, as a dictator, unjustly forced His law and rule on the angels who would have a better life apart from Him? What if the charges were that God in jealousy forced Satan from heaven?

If Satan made these charges against God, and God immediately destroyed Satan, the onlooking universe might wonder if Satan's charges were valid. So the universe rivets its attention here to the earth as Satan and God each reveal how their government works. This world serves the role of a petri dish, allowing the cultures of sin and righteousness to grow until the inhabitants of the universe can recognize the true character of each side. Paul explains, "For we are made a spectacle unto the world, and to angels, and to men" (1 Corinthians 4:9, KJV). We take center stage on the theater of the universe. Here God permits Satan space enough to demonstrate his plan and his heart.

God did not create a devil

Satan wasn't always an evil antagonist; his glory once shone in harmony with Yahweh's as the morning star, "son of the dawn" (Isaiah 14:12). He once served in the direct presence of God as a covering cherub and one of the angelic bodyguard (Ezekiel 28:14). With such an impressive angelic being, we can understand why angels were taken by his beauty and power and the role God had given him.

This magnificently created being nurtured selfishness in his own heart, breeding sin that would soon pass to his followers. His pride dethroned the Lord from his life as he maneuvered to exalt self to the status of Godhood (Isaiah 14:14). Sin entered the universe when love gave way to selfishness. This campaign of innuendo, supposition, and doubt drew a contingency of angels to this tainted yet beautiful leader of the angel host. He would not be reasoned with, and he led a revolt in heaven.

War broke out, and Michael (the Son of God) led the loyal angelic host and cast the dragonlike serpent Satan to the earth with his demonic host. The devil strategized that his way back to the throne will be gained through the worship of mankind. So he seeks to trick humans into separating themselves from God, because only as they make themselves enemies of God do they lose His protection.

Satan seeks to incite mankind to reject God. John exposes that it is the devil, not God, who placed the desire to betray Jesus into Judas's heart (John 13:2). That makes perfect sense, since James assures mankind that God "cannot be tempted by evil, and He Himself does not tempt anyone" (James 1:13). Once Satan separates a person from God, he then seeks to destroy him or her just as he brought Judas to the place of suicide.

Four additional concepts vindicate God

As extensions of the great controversy between God and Satan, four additional concepts help us to understand God's character in the light of pain, suffering, and evil.

1. God gave humanity the freedom to choose righteousness and love or choose the opposite. When humans chose to separate from God and put Satan as their leader, their nature became distorted. Selfishness became ingrained in human DNA. So now, not only does Satan tempt mankind to evil, "but each one is tempted when he is carried away and enticed by his own lust. Then when lust has conceived, it gives birth to sin; and when sin is accomplished, it brings forth death" (James 1:14, 15).

Shouldn't we recognize that we as humans played a part in bringing pain and suffering upon ourselves and others? When we hear about a mugging, a rape, or a mass murder, we have another place to put blame. Our promiscuity breeds STDs, addicts steal, the abused repeat the cycle of abuse, and drunk drivers kill. The pain in these real-life examples comes as a result of humans' corrupt nature, and it helps us to grasp the end results of allowing Satan to reign in our hearts.

2. God stands alone as the source of life. He not only grants us life, He Himself is the essence of that life. God claims, "I am the way, and the truth and the life" (John 14:6). God sustains all life with His being. Sometimes we judge God's justice and mercy based on how long we, or others, get to live on this earth—an assessment that comes from a limited understanding. Practically, we view this present existence as real life and what comes after as an elusive possibility.

God, on the other hand, has the bigger perspective of eternal life. "I am the resurrection and the life; he who believes in Me will live even if he dies, and everyone who lives and believes in Me will never die" (John 11:25, 26). Since He grants all the opportunity for eternal life, does that not compensate for His limiting the time we spend on this earth with its sin, suffering, and heartache? When we determine someone's life has ended early or that they died young, can we assume God has been unfair? Does it matter if He gives one person ten dollars *now* and another person one hundred dollars *now* if He ultimately offers both of them unlimited money?

Have we earned the right to live even one hour? So if He grants to one person seventy years upon this earth and to another seventy days, who am I to challenge His gift? *Any amount of life we receive demonstrates God's generosity.*

3. God wants everyone to be saved. When we review the problem of suffering, we might remember that "the Lord is . . . not wishing for any to perish but for all to come to repentance" (2 Peter 3:9). He has provided a way that every single being upon this earth can live forever with Him through the death of Jesus. Not everyone will choose God and the life He has provided, but that will not reflect on God's justice. Ultimately, God will honor our choice.

God will use the pain, suffering, grief, and heartache for the purpose of bringing broken humanity and the onlooking universe back into harmony with Him. As Christians, we deal with the pain of this life as a short, momentary affliction compared with the ultimate reality of eternity with God.

I must understand that God doesn't just care about me. He cares about my wife, my children, my neighbors, and my enemies. So He may allow pain in my life for the sake of bringing someone else to Him. As a father, if I see that one of my children might be saved by watching me go through an early death with cancer while trusting in God, then I would not only endure it, I would beg for it. If suffering financial loss would keep me humble and dependent and seeking God, I pray to God, "Keep me poor."

4. God takes sin upon Himself. God suffered for our sin. "He made Him who knew no sin to be sin on our behalf, so that we might become the righteousness of God in Him" (2 Corinthians 5:21). "The Lord has caused the iniquity of us all to fall on Him" (Isaiah 53:6).

A compassionate Father still exists in the midst of suffering

At times, when we suffer or someone dies, we shake our fists at heaven and insist that God has failed us. We see the atrocities committed on humanity by humanity, and we question what sort of God could be behind it. Where is God?

We have discovered that many elements factor into the answer. We understand that Satan authored pain, suffering, and death. The great controversy reveals that God has allowed this demonstration of what the world would be like under the prince of darkness. And we recognize that apart from God, wickedness reigns in humans' hearts.

Let me add the perspective of a father. I have held my crying baby in my arms as the doctors gave her shots to save her life. I cried with her in the pain. It seemed her tears begged me to intervene, but I knew that going through the pain was necessary for her future. So I held her as we both cried. I soothed her as best as I could. Though she may doubt I cared because I didn't spare her the pain, I ached with her pain, and my heart was drawn even more to her because of her suffering.

So where is God in the midst of my pain? He holds me in His arms in my suffering and records each tear that falls. He will not let me suffer even a moment of needless pain. When I feel like a victim held captive by an abuser and question God's care for me in my pain, I catch a glimpse of the torture instrument of the cross. I want to cover His nakedness to spare Him from the humiliation. I instinctively feel like putting my face in my hands to avoid witnessing the pain of His ripped flesh, impaled hands, perforated side, and His broken heart. But I cannot turn away, because in the midst of all of this horrific terror I comprehend the depth of His love for me. And to the question in my heart, "Where are You, God?" I hear Him whisper, "Here on the cross, taking your place." Then my heart flows with joy as, behind the scenes, I find a God beyond my wildest dreams!

Thoughts to Ponder

1. How does Job's story help me to understand the problem of pain? Can I, like Job, trust God's heart even when I don't understand the leading of His hand?

_____

_____

_____

2. What would I list as the biggest suffering in my life? How has pain or suffering in my life shaped my view of God's character?

_____

_____

_____

3. Have I consciously or unconsciously blamed God for Satan's actions?

_____

_____

_____

4. How does realizing everything comes to me "Father filtered" give me hope in difficult circumstances?

_____

_____

_____

5. Have I judged God based on how long someone lives on earth? Does my belief in a heavenly eternity give me a different perspective on suffering?

_____

_____

_____

CHAPTER 3

The God Who Came to Earth

She couldn't shelter Him forever. He must have heard it from the other kids as He played in the hills of Nazareth: "Joseph isn't your real daddy, is he?" "You don't know who your daddy is, do you?" "No, he was born of a sunbeam like Tammuz." Whether Joseph and Mary were proactive or shared the circumstances of Jesus' birth as a response to outside pressures, Jesus must have known early on that He was different. Although part of a big family with unnamed sisters and four brothers—James, Judas, Joseph, and Simon—His birth made Him unique (Luke 8:19; Matthew 13:55, 56; Mark 6:3).

Only in mythology had a God-man existed. Unlike the mythical story of Hercules—with the god Zeus impregnating Alcmene, thereby creating a god—Jesus preexisted as God. Mary must have shared with her Son that the Holy Spirit had come over her, and He was both human and God. She must have explained the mission of the Messiah as she understood it and rehearsed the scriptures again and again, pointing Him to His divine mission.

Part of the Trinity

Jesus accepted a mission of divine origin. He came to earth as God in the flesh. God the Almighty Father and the Holy Spirit were in Christ "reconciling the world" to themselves (2 Corinthians 5:19). Even though Jesus limited Himself and joined with humanity, He retained His divinity (Philippians 2:6, 7). Though they all bear the same nature—all-loving, self-sacrificing, all-knowing, immortal, holy, multipresent, and all-powerful—Jesus took the role of coming to earth and fusing with human flesh. The one God in three personages, beyond comprehension, not only sought to reveal His character to the people He created, but to rescue mankind. The Godhead together formed the plan for Jesus to come to earth before the earth's creation (1 Peter 1:20; Revelation 13:8).

The mission of the God-man

Jesus needed a God-human nature to complete His mission. He embarked on a multifaceted mission all with the same purpose: to restore sinners to a holy God. "Christ Jesus came into the world to save sinners" (1 Timothy 1:15).

Jesus' mission is as follows:

To validate and reveal God's character. Jesus came to reveal the Father to us. "Nor does anyone know the Father except the Son, and anyone to whom the Son wills to reveal Him" (Matthew 11:27). He would need to join with humanity to demonstrate that God

This chapter is based on Seventh-day Adventist fundamental beliefs no. 2, "The Trinity"; and no. 4, "The Son."

had been fair in His original creation. That man, as originally created from God's hand, could live the precepts of the law. This would squelch the charges Satan might make against God—that Adam and Eve could not have passed the test of obedience He gave them. God, becoming a human to rescue us, also demonstrated the value He has placed on us.

To become our substitute. "Christ redeemed us from the curse of the Law, having become a curse for us—for it is written, 'CURSED IS EVERYONE WHO HANGS ON A TREE' " (Galatians 3:13). To become our substitute, He needed to live a perfect human life joined to God. That life must be without sin, and deserving of eternal life, in order to have a perfect life to exchange for our sinful lives. "Just as the Son of Man did not come to be served, but to serve, and to give His life a ransom for many" (Matthew 20:28).

We can understand events in Jesus' life from a totally new perspective when we understand that He lived a life as an example for us. His baptism has nothing to do with the remission of His own sin, since He had no sin (1 Peter 1:21; 2 Corinthians 5:21). But everyone who joins themselves to Jesus receives His life. The thief on the cross received Jesus' flawless life, and His baptism was put to his account. For this reason, when John the Baptist protested that the sinless Jesus didn't need baptism, Jesus responded, "Permit it at this time; for in this way it is fitting for us to fulfill *all* righteousness" (Matthew 3:15; emphasis added).

To become our example. "Christ also suffered for you, leaving you an example for you to follow in His steps" (1 Peter 2:21). I can hear the command to forgive, but it is in seeing Jesus demonstrate forgiveness to those who stripped Him naked, beat Him, and crucified Him on the cross that forgiveness becomes real. As He prays, "Father, forgive them; for they do not know what they are doing" (Luke 23:34), forgiveness becomes tangible. Watching people perfectly live out their connection with God in their relationships inspires me to live similarly. Jesus' humanity provides me with an additional connection to Him. I have someone who understands, who also has been through the struggle. Jesus became "a merciful and faithful high priest in things pertaining to God" (Hebrews 2:17).

To destroy the works of the devil. "The Son of God appeared for this purpose, to destroy the works of the devil" (1 John 3:8). "Only as a human being could he die, and only by dying could he break the power of the devil, who had the power of death" (Hebrews 2:14, NLT). Jesus defeats Satan: "Now judgment is upon this world; now the ruler of this world will be cast out" (John 12:31). He resists temptation as a human being, and Jesus claims "the ruler of the world is coming, and he has nothing in Me" (John 14:30). By dying He conquers death. "But now has been revealed by the appearing of our Savior Christ Jesus, who abolished death and brought life and immortality to light through the gospel" (2 Timothy 1:10).

To become our advocate. Like the high priest of old, Jesus came to connect earth and heaven. Having lived in both worlds, His life acts as a bridge between divinity and humanity. He is our Advocate. "Therefore, He had to be made like His brethren in all things, so that He might become a merciful and faithful high priest in things pertaining to God, to make propitiation for the sins of the people. For since He Himself was tempted in that which He has suffered, He is able to come to the aid of those who are tempted" (Hebrews 2:17, 18).

During Jesus' first trip to Jerusalem, at the age of twelve, He watched sinners lay their hands on the lamb and slit its throat and He recognized it as the symbol of His mission.

Later, on the trip home, when His parents realized that He was missing, they returned to Jerusalem and found Him in the temple. When they questioned Him about His absence, He responded, "Did you not know that I had to be in My Father's house?" (Luke 2:49). The King James Version translates Jesus' response as "that I must be about my Father's business." The two words *house* and *business* are trying to interpret the Greek words by some English idiom. Literally Jesus says, "Did you not know I had to be in the things that are My Father's?" He said this to His earthly father about His heavenly Father. Even at a tender young age, His heart was tuned to His Father's plan. At the age of twelve, Jesus knew He was God's Son with a mission.

Fully man

To complete this mission of rescue, Jesus took on a human nature weakened from four thousand years of sin, complete with the infirmities of the human race present in His time. Jesus took on humanity after the race had decreased in physical stamina and in moral strength to resist sin. Yet Christ stood against Satan's temptations. "For we do not have a high priest who cannot sympathize with our weaknesses, but One who has been tempted in all things as we are, yet without sin" (Hebrews 4:15). He became the Second Adam, a corporate representative of mankind.

Though He was tempted, He had no sin. Some have wondered how Scripture could accurately express that Jesus was tempted in "all things" when He could not have each of our specific temptations. He was never tempted to extravagance or vanity by a new red Ferrari. Not being married, He was never tempted to cheat on His wife. Never having committed a sin, He was never tempted to recommit a former sin.

Some argue that because Jesus was born at a point in time, and to a specific class, He cannot have every specific temptation we have. Then how was He tempted in all ways as we are? The basis for temptation is to distrust God and rely on self. Jesus was tempted to turn from obedience and submission to God for what He might perceive to be self-gain.

Some would argue that Jesus had an unfair advantage over us, in that He doesn't have to fight an overwhelming inclination to sin. But He also had temptations that we do not have. How many of us have been tempted to turn stones into bread, or call a legion of angels to destroy our enemies? I could argue that none of us have resisted sin to the point of sweating blood, let alone "to the point of death" (Philippians 2:8). But these arguments miss the issue.

While Jesus did come to show us an example, He did more by paying a price in becoming our substitute. The issue is not, can we live like Jesus? The issue is this: was Jesus' link to humanity sufficient to save our lives? We do not compete with Jesus to save our own lives. Jesus took on humanity ultimately to redeem us. In His unique humanity, He offered Himself as a ransom. His humanity must be different than ours because we require a Savior. Jesus proved Satan wrong: a human, as He came from God's hand, can live a perfect life. Jesus conquered death. He links Himself to us forever. He sets an example of how humans, filled with the Holy Spirit, can live.

God in the flesh understands being hungry, hurting, getting sick, and being bone tired. He experienced being misunderstood, rejected, and betrayed. He cried, felt disappointment, was amazed, and got angry. He had to deal with corrupt human authority and deal with the everyday struggles of finances. Jesus' birth as a common carpenter instead of a rich royal king helps us know He understands dealing with the humblest circumstances.

From the beginning, He knew that He came to this earth in order to die. That He took on humanity for the purpose of laying down His life. So when I see Him steadily moving toward the cross, and experiencing the suffering, I say with Pilate, "Behold, the Man!" (John 19:5).

Fully God

Jesus claimed to be God. While being fully aware of His humanity, Jesus had no doubt about His divinity. When the Jewish leaders questioned Him about who He was, "Jesus said to them, 'Truly, truly, I say to you, before Abraham was born, I am.' Therefore they picked up stones to throw at Him, but Jesus hid Himself and went out of the temple" (John 8:58, 59). Jesus knew that He existed with the Father before the world was made. "Now, Father, glorify Me together with Yourself, with the glory which I had with You before the world was" (John 17:5). In Isaiah 42:8, God said, "I am the Lord; that is My name; I will not give My glory to another, nor My praise to graven images." The Lord would not give His glory to anyone else. That Jesus possessed this glory with the Father from the beginning shows He was united with the Father as a coeternal personage of the Godhead.

Jesus claimed the ability to give eternal life (John 10:28). He claimed that He and the Father "are one" (John 10:30). He shared not only that His followers needed to believe in Him to have eternal life but that He is the source of that life. "Jesus said to [Martha], 'I am the resurrection and the life; he who believes in Me will live even if he dies' " (John 11:25). Jesus delineates that He is not just a messenger for life but that He is life itself. No true prophet or angel could ever make such a claim. Jesus could truly say, "I am the way, and the truth, and the life" (John 14:6).

Jesus received worship. Jesus knew that only God deserved worship. During the temptation in the wilderness, He stated, "Go, Satan! For it is written, 'You shall worship the Lord your God, and serve Him only' " (Matthew 4:10). So when Jesus accepted worship, He did so knowing that it is the prerogative of God alone. "And those who were in the boat worshiped Him, saying, 'You are certainly God's Son!' " (Matthew 14:33). Mere created beings could not accept worship. It was forbidden (Romans 1:25). Even angels, though heavenly beings, would not receive worship, which is due only to God (Revelation 19:10). Jesus recognized that He was God.

Jesus forgave sins. Jesus healed a paralytic, but that doesn't prove His divinity; prophets did that as well. But Jesus used the miracle of healing to call for the Father's testimony that "the Son of Man has authority on earth to forgive sins" (Mark 2:10). These scribes realized that only God has the power to forgive sins, so they assumed Jesus was blaspheming against God Almighty (Mark 2:7). Jesus was not merely explaining how God the Father forgives sins or what the conditions were for forgiveness of sin. He was claiming His own authority as God to forgive sin.

The Father testifies to Jesus' divinity

On the mount of transfiguration as Jesus announced that He would go to Jerusalem to die for the sins of the world, the Father stated His approval: "While [Peter] was still speaking, a bright cloud overshadowed them, and behold, a voice out of the cloud said, 'This is My beloved Son, with whom I am well-pleased; listen to Him!' " (Matthew 17:5). As it is stated in John 3:16, "For this is how God loved the world: He gave his uniquely existing Son so that everyone who believes in him would not be lost but have eternal life" (ISV). Jesus is *the unique, one-of-a-kind* Son of God. Though we all may become children of God, He is the one Son (John 1:2).

In this case, calling Jesus *Son* does not indicate physical birth; instead, it describes someone with similar characteristics. For example, "sons of light" is used to indicate those who are shining with the characteristics of truth and purity (1 Thessalonians 5:5). And the phrase "son of wickedness" found in Psalm 89:22 is used to indicate those living a wicked life. Jesus possessed the exact character of His heavenly Father so much so that Jesus could tell His disciples, "He who has seen Me has seen the Father" (John 14:9).

God clearly indicates that Jesus was not a son formed by birth or creation; otherwise, He could not be God. " 'You are My witnesses,' declares the Lord, 'and My servant whom I have chosen, so that you may know and believe Me and understand that I am He. Before Me there was no God formed, and there will be none after Me' " (Isaiah 43:10). If Jesus did not preexist as God, He would have come after the Father and therefore would not be coeternal or coequal with the Father. Jesus' title "Son of God" does not designate Him as a created being but one fully possessing the attributes of God Almighty. He is fully God, not merely a created being.

Jesus is equal to Yahweh

Jesus calls us to witness for Him, just as Yahweh did in the Old Testament (Acts 1:6–8; Isaiah 43:10). Both Yahweh and Jesus claim the title "The first and the last" (Isaiah 44:6; Revelation 22:13–16). But these claims are only the beginning.

Paul declares that you must confess Jesus is Lord to be saved. "If you confess with your mouth Jesus as Lord, and believe in your heart that God raised Him from the dead, you will be saved; for with the heart a person believes, resulting in righteousness, and with the mouth he confesses, resulting in salvation. For the Scripture says, 'Whoever believes in Him will not be disappointed.' For there is no distinction between Jew and Greek; for the same Lord is Lord of all, abounding in riches for all who call on Him; for 'Whoever will call on the name of the Lord will be saved' " (Romans 10:9–13).

Here Paul quotes Joel 2:32, "And everyone who calls on the name of the Lord will be saved" (NIV). In most Bible translations, when you see "Lord" or "God" in small capital letters, it indicates that the original language refers to the personal name of God.

This special name of God is represented by the letters YHWH. It is sometimes written *Yahweh* or *Jehovah* so we can read it. The Jews considered the name of God to be too sacred to pronounce. In the original Hebrew language, only consonants were used. When speaking, they replaced YHWH with *Adonai*, the general name for God or Lord.

Since God's name was considered so special, it is thrilling to see Jesus indicated as

"Lᴏʀᴅ" in a text using God's personal name to validate that claim. The heavenly Father gave to Jesus the name *Immanuel*, which means "God with us" (Matthew 1:23, NIV).

Jesus was and is fully God. He recognized Himself as God while He was on earth. He accepted worship, granted forgiveness, claimed eternal existence, and presented Himself as the source of life. As Creator, Jesus deserves the worship of His creatures. The Father validated Jesus' claims by speaking from heaven.

That a God would take on lowly humanity to save sinful, rebellious children reveals a God beyond my wildest dreams.

Thoughts to Ponder

1. What purpose do I usually ascribe to Jesus' coming? What purpose most easily evades me?

2. In what areas do I find comfort that Jesus understands experientially what I am going through?

3. While on earth, Jesus remained God. What difference does it make to me? If Jesus lived fully as God, what does it tell me about how God wants to relate to me?

4. What feelings might Jesus have experienced in leaving heaven and lowering Himself to come to earth? What did He lose? What would motivate me to be willing to experience such loss?

5. Jesus knew His mission. What mission has God given me? Am I living my life totally for that mission?

CHAPTER 4

The Warrior Coach

Simon was baptized along with almost everyone else in town. We would have called the new convert a magician, though some thought he was more than that. He dazzled the city with his supposed power; the crowd attributed these spectacular acts to supernatural powers. Surely he held to the ancient magicians' code of never telling anyone the mysteries behind his sleight of hand, received as a legacy from his father.

Sorcerer, warlock, or con man, this showman had convinced the populace of his greatness. Dazzled by his abilities, people called him "the Great Power" or the "Great Wizard." While the truth of the gospel convicted Simon to choose Jesus, he still craved attention and self-glorification.

When Peter and John arrived in Samaria, they instantly reached superstar status. Joining Philip the evangelist, they laid hands on the people and prayed, and the Holy Spirit entered people's lives. "When Simon saw that the Spirit was given at the laying on of the apostles' hands, he offered them money and said, 'Give me also this ability so that everyone on whom I lay my hands may receive the Holy Spirit' " (Acts 8:18, 19, NIV).

Simon didn't want the Holy Spirit to use him—instead, he wanted to use the Spirit. Many times the Holy Spirit has been sought as a shortcut to fulfilling our desires for power, pleasure, perfection, and perception. Jesus' apostles answered Simon, saying, "May your money perish with you, because you thought you could buy the gift of God with money! You have no part or share in this ministry, because your heart is not right before God. Repent of this wickedness and pray to the Lord in the hope that he may forgive you for having such a thought in your heart. For I see that you are full of bitterness and captive to sin" (Acts 8:20–23, NIV).

Simon's sin? His corruption consisted of misusing the Holy Spirit; self still took center stage in Simon's life. I must pause to ask myself, How much of my desire to be Spirit filled stems from a self-serving motive?

Using the Holy Spirit as a shortcut

Just as many people would rather take a pill to get thin than exercise, eat right, and get enough sleep, so we sometimes see the Holy Spirit as a spiritual shortcut to spare us the process and work of inner growth.

The Holy Spirit a shortcut to power. They clamor after the Spirit for self-exaltation, not because of an inner desire for harmony with God. They command and demand the Spirit

This chapter is based on Seventh-day Adventist fundamental belief no. 5, "The Holy Spirit."

37

instead of yielding to Him. They claim they receive healings, miracles, demon exorcisms, and financial blessings from Him.

The Holy Spirit a shortcut to pleasure. Some people insist that the Holy Spirit give to them good feelings and a prosperous life. They crave the rush His presence brings like an addict longs for his next fix. The Spirit becomes their pleasure pill. They expect the Spirit to not only bring instant pleasure and ecstasy but also spiritual assurance. They claim this as evidence that God validates and approves their life.

The Holy Spirit a shortcut to perception. Some also use the Holy Spirit as a shortcut to discern God's will, expecting Him to lead by emotional impressions, signs, and wonders. They look to their version of the Holy Spirit as a substitute for Bible study and prayer.

The Holy Spirit a shortcut to perfection. Looking for a shortcut to having a good standing with God, many expect the Spirit to give them instantaneous victory. They assume He will spare them from the pain of resisting temptation.

Taking a rain check on the Holy Spirit

In response to the charismatic movement, many fundamental Christians try to avoid emotionalism and end up putting the work of the Holy Spirit on the back burner. They hold onto the impersonal doctrine of the Holy Spirit, like holding onto a rain check, knowing that sometime soon the product will come in. They wait for the genuine latter rain outpouring of the Spirit, when they will exchange their ticket for the real article. They worship dispassionately, debate religious ideas, and serve out of duty (with no joy), while they hold the Holy Spirit at arm's length.

Wanting the Holy Spirit

These two extremes call us to choose between an impersonal force that we can command and an impersonal doctrine that we give intellectual assent to—but has little to do with our everyday experience.

Is it wrong to seek the Holy Spirit? Have you wanted personal power? Do you want to belong to a church where people aren't snoring in the pews but are energized, alive, vibrant, and even on fire? Have you wanted an experience to lift you above the everyday doldrums? Have you wanted to see, to feel, to touch God? Have you dreamed of the power of God being evident in you?

I want more of the Holy Spirit in my life; I long to feel what others have claimed to feel. I want His Spirit to touch my spirit and move me. I want God to use me to heal others. Above everything else I want God to direct me for His work. And above every other desire, I want to do God's will and serve Him. I will seek the Spirit to do the work that God wants done in my life.

I want to answer the question I brought up at the beginning of this section. Is it wrong to seek the Holy Spirit? Godly men and women pursue the Holy Spirit. If we long after Him, as the living God, we honor God's will for us.

The Holy Spirit resides in us

The Bible pictures the Holy Spirit in a unique role. "But the Counselor, the Holy Spirit, whom the Father will send in my name, he will teach you all things, and bring to your remembrance all that I have said to you" (John 14:26, RSV). The word translated "Counselor" in this passage comes from the Greek term *Paraclete*. This word refers to a companion coach in battle.

Picture yourself being called into battle. You immediately find yourself dealing with a life-or-death situation—yours. The battle rages between the ruler of the dark domain and the Prince of Righteousness. You face the future with a terrible foreboding.

Then everything changes—the Warrior Coach comes as your personal trainer and companion, to aid you as you fight through the battle together. He encourages, challenges, instructs, and guides you through the minefields. He commits Himself to bringing you back home.

He trains you, equips you, fights by your side, and interprets the high command's orders. When you feel beaten down, weak, and vulnerable, He stands in the gap as your protector. When you are wounded in battle, He carries you and nurses you back to health. With Him at your side, you fear no evil, and you feel secure that you will complete your mission.

The battle Satan launched against Christ positions him as our enemy, yet he tries to coax us to his side. When that fails, he launches an all-out attack to destroy us. The Warrior Coach knows his tactic and empowers us to hold our ground.

The Holy Spirit often works quietly—behind the scenes—not calling attention to Himself. He transforms people's lives by the quiet inside work of convicting the conscience. Elijah discovered that this personal God neither thundered in a mighty wind, nor shook the ground in a devastating earthquake, nor flashed Himself in the bright flaming fire, but spoke in the still, small Voice (1 Kings 19:9–13). The Holy Spirit is not some new discovery in modern days. Let's review how the Spirit has worked in the past, and with whom, in order to better understand how He wants to work today.

The Holy Spirit lived actively in the Old Testament
Scripture introduces Him as the active God in creation: "Now the earth was formless and empty, darkness was over the surface of the deep, and the Spirit of God was hovering over the waters" (Genesis 1:2, NIV). The Holy Spirit acted not only in creation; He functioned throughout the Old Testament. He was poured out on Moses and the seventy during the Exodus (Numbers 11:25). He provided Gideon's power and strengthened Samson (Judges 6:34; 14:19). He moved King Saul to prophesy, and King David pleaded for Him not to leave him (1 Samuel 11:6; Psalm 51:11).

The Old Testament promised that the Spirit would come in an even more powerful way. "And afterward, I will pour out my Spirit on all people. Your sons and daughters will prophesy, your old men will dream dreams, your young men will see visions. Even on my servants, both men and women, I will pour out my Spirit in those days" (Joel 2:28, 29, NIV). The focus of the Holy Spirit's work on priests, kings, and judges moves to the common believer. Young and old, male and female, all may receive the promised Holy Spirit.

How can I receive the Holy Spirit?

Receiving the Holy Spirit means opening myself to allow Him to do His work in my life. What work does the Spirit seek to accomplish in my life? He seeks to teach me as a counselor (John 14:26). Jesus tell us, "When the Counselor comes, . . . he will bear witness to me" (John 15:26, RSV).

He will give us power to "put to death the misdeeds of the body" (Romans 8:13, NIV). He will give us assurance of our standing with God. "The Spirit himself testifies with our spirit that we are God's children" (Romans 8:16, NIV). He conveys our heart to the Father when we don't have the words (Romans 8:26). We will find "righteousness, peace and joy in the Holy Spirit" (Romans 14:17, NIV). He helps us lose sight of ourselves and empowers us to serve others. "Now to each one the manifestation of the Spirit is given for the common good" (1 Corinthians 12:7, NIV).

Who can receive the Spirit?

The Spirit *works* on every heart, moving people to surrender their lives, but He can only *live* in the life that willingly obeys God. "We are witnesses of these things, and so is the Holy Spirit, whom God has given to those who obey him" (Acts 5:32, NIV). When we surrender, the Holy Spirit works on us and resides in us. "Peter replied, 'Repent and be baptized, every one of you, in the name of Jesus Christ for the forgiveness of your sins. And you will receive the gift of the Holy Spirit' " (Acts 2:38, NIV).

We must accept Jesus as Lord in order to receive the Spirit. "On the last and greatest day of the festival, Jesus stood and said in a loud voice, 'Let anyone who is thirsty come to me and drink. Whoever believes in me, as Scripture has said, rivers of living water will flow from within them.' By this he meant the Spirit, whom those who believed in him were later to receive. Up to that time the Spirit had not been given, since Jesus had not yet been glorified" (John 7:37–39, NIV). Before Christ's crucifixion, the Holy Spirit had not yet been experienced in His fullness, but that does not mean that the Holy Spirit had not been working. "The Spirit of truth . . . the world cannot receive, because it does not see Him or know Him, but you know Him because He abides with you and will be in you" (John 14:17).

Christ has provided salvation for everyone, but only those who accept His gift will benefit from it. In the same way, the Spirit draws everyone but will only live in those who yield to Him by accepting Jesus. He fills us as we yield our lives to Him. The disciples had the Holy Spirit *with* them, and He would be *in* them. After His resurrection and just before His return to heaven, Jesus told His disciples to wait and they would receive power from the Holy Spirit. "But you will receive power when the Holy Spirit comes on you; and you will be my witnesses in Jerusalem, and in all Judea and Samaria, and to the ends of the earth" (Acts 1:8, NIV).

The Spirit's work in me

The Holy Spirit does not seek to glorify me but to glorify God through me. The Spirit calls me to crucify self so that I can be connected with God. Jesus described the work of the Holy Spirit: "When he comes, he will prove the world to be in the wrong about sin and righteousness and judgment: about sin, because people do not believe in me" (John 16:8, 9, NIV). As we grow to trust Jesus more, we will despise sin.

Convicting me of sin

With the Holy Spirit working in my life, I can no longer ignore the reality of my sin. He convicts me of my sin, and I am brought to own the choices I have made. He unmasks the folly of sin, so that when I analyze it I find it irrational and know that it destroys my life. Sin goes against my best interest. He helps me to realize the filth of sin. I see it in contrast to all that is pure, and it begins to disgust me. He exposes the fact that sin permeates my very nature. The Holy Spirit also points out the fruit of sin—unhappiness, discord, loneliness, pain, and ultimately death. When I have allowed the Spirit to convict me of the change I need in my life, then He works in me the power to live. We live victoriously when we see that sin deeply hurts our best Friend, Christ. We no longer avoid sin merely because of rules but to protect a precious relationship with Jesus.

Convicting me of righteousness

When Christ went to the Father, we no longer had a visible standard of righteousness. The Spirit works to confront us with Christ's righteousness, exposing our own righteousness as filthy rags. The Spirit convicts me of the insufficiency of my righteousness and strips away any pretense of gaining eternal life on my merits. Calvary shows me a standard of holiness that would not be compromised.

I receive the assurance that Christ's righteousness becomes mine as He lives in and through me. The issue of righteousness no longer focuses on my righteousness but the righteousness of the Christ who lives in and through me.

Convicting me of judgment

Too often I think of the Holy Spirit only in the first phase, when He convicts me of sin. However, the Holy Spirit also convicts me concerning judgment, and not only my judgment, but also God's judgment upon Satan. "And about judgment, because the prince of this world now stands condemned" (John 16:11, NIV).

God defeated Satan on the cross. The death blow has already been delivered.

God broke Satan's rule over mankind. He no longer has a right to control us. We don't have to be bullied.

I do not have to defeat Satan; God won the battle for me. I fight the battle of staying connected to Christ. I am free to choose God and the power He provides. We can share with others that we all have a choice; and we can say, "As for me and my household, we will serve the LORD" (Joshua 24:15, NIV).

The Holy Spirit brings fruit

With the Holy Spirit in control of their lives, converts live differently than those who are not saved. They daily sacrifice their selfish nature; they live crucified. No longer do they live but Christ lives in them.

The fruit of the union with the Holy Spirit "is love, joy, peace, patience, kindness, goodness, faithfulness, gentleness and self-control. Against such things there is no law. Those who belong to Christ Jesus have crucified the flesh with its passions and desires" (Galatians 5:22–24, NIV). The disciples rejoiced and praised Jesus with a loud voice, and

Jesus approved (Luke 19:37–40). It is right to express our love and joy. If we didn't praise Him, the rocks would cry out (Luke 19:40).

The Bible tells us that thousands were converted in a day at the outpouring of the Holy Spirit. Today the outpouring of the Holy Spirit has led to more people giving their hearts to God than when Christ walked upon the earth.

There are no shortcuts. Those who receive the Holy Spirit in power to witness must first receive the Holy Spirit as He transforms the heart and empties it of its selfishness.

Sometimes people ask, "Are you a Spirit-filled, born-again Christian?" They make it sound as though Holy Spirit–filled Christians form an elite or super level of Christianity, a sort of Christian deluxe. All Christians by nature must be Spirit filled. Paul declares in Romans, "If anyone does not have the Spirit of Christ, they do not belong to Christ" (Romans 8:9, NIV).

God the Holy Spirit resides in us as our personal God. Like a Warrior Coach, He takes care of us. He confronts us with our sin, with Christ's righteousness, and with Satan's defeat in judgment, and walks with us through the battlefield of life. He comforts us when we need a pick-me-up and convicts us when we need to move off the pew. He performs all of His work to bring us into unity with Jesus. Having God as my personal Warrior Coach—now that is a God beyond my wildest dreams!

Thoughts to Ponder

1. Like Simon, have I tried to use the Holy Spirit for my purposes rather than yield to His purposes in my life? Have I sensed others were doing that?

_____

_____

_____

2. If I were to use the Holy Spirit as a shortcut, what would I be most likely to use Him for—power, pleasure, perception, or perfection?

_____

_____

_____

3. How does the image of the Warrior Coach impact me emotionally? What do I need most from Him in the battle against Satan?

_____

_____

_____

4. Have I feared the work of the Holy Spirit in my life? Have I sensed His Spirit testifying to my spirit that He lives present in me?

_____

_____

_____

5. Who would I count as the most Spirit-filled Christian that I know? What evidences make me believe this person is Spirit filled?

_____

_____

_____

CHAPTER 5

Spiritual Fusion

For the purposes of this chapter, let's look at this brief working definition of *fusion*: the merging of different elements into union; or, to intricately join two or more elements together so that the parts become a new whole. The word seems to carry the connotation of joining together things that were deemed impossible to merge. Scientists talk of two basic forms of fusion: thermonuclear fusion, which uses high temperatures to fuse the nuclei of atoms; and the controversial cold fusion (dismissed by some as a delusional fantasy), which uses a low-temperature process to theoretically accomplish the same end product.

Why am I talking of fusion? Because I unexpectedly stumbled upon the concept of spiritual fusion in the Bible: "Anyone who is joined to Christ is a new being; the old is gone, the new has come" (2 Corinthians 5:17, GNT).

Other versions translate "joined to Christ" as "in Christ" (NIV), "belongs to Christ" (NLT), and "is a believer in Christ" (GW). These all carry the same point: the two become a new whole. We do not just believe in Jesus or His teachings; we merge with Christ. Paul uses similar phrases: "in Him," "in the beloved," "through Him," and "in whom" throughout his writings to explain what happens when Jesus lives in a believer as Lord.

Marinated or pickled Christians
One day while cooking for an upcoming Hawaiian luau, I discovered a practical example of fusion. I made a marinade of barbecue sauce, pineapple juice, teriyaki sauce, and soy sauce and soaked kabobs in the sauce overnight. The next day, when guests bit into them, they raved about the infused taste—the kabobs were not just covered with sauce, they had absorbed the rich flavor of the sauce. The Christian experience resembles marinated kabobs. We live in Christ to the point that we take on the flavor of His love.

I might also compare Christian fusion to pickled Christians. No, I am not speaking about the sour attitude some Christians have reflected in their scowl, but rather I refer to the process of pickling. When a tender young cucumber has been soaked in vinegar and dill, we refer to it as a new creation, a pickle. The cucumber has been changed; pickling alters the very properties of its color, consistency, and taste. In Christ we become something new and different. We don't just wear a covering of Christ; He permeates our being and transforms us into something new.

This chapter is based on Seventh-day Adventist fundamental beliefs no. 11, "Growing in Christ";
no. 15, "Baptism"; and no. 16, "The Lord's Supper."

Both sanctified and being sanctified

God "in us" sanctifies us. "By that will we *have been* sanctified through the offering of the body of Jesus Christ once for all" (Hebrews 10:10, NKJV; emphasis added). God offered Jesus as a "once and for all" sacrifice, and by it we "have been sanctified"—past tense, already complete. Jesus does not keep paying for our sin. He does not need to offer Himself for sin again and again. Every sin that will ever be committed God has, from His side, already covered and therefore forgiven. He offered "one sacrifice for sins" (Hebrews 10:12).

I am *already* sanctified by what Jesus has done, and at the same time I am growing daily in Christ. Can I simultaneously "be perfected" for all time and be "in the process of being made holy"? Paul explains that we hold both standings simultaneously: "For by one offering He *has perfected* forever those who *are being* sanctified" (Hebrew 10:14, NKJV; emphasis added).

Christ paid the price that set us free from Satan's bondage. Joining with Christ, I receive all His righteousness on my account, while at the same time He increasingly lives His righteousness through me.

God paid the price for *all* of mankind's sin, whether we accept it or not. From His side, He covers sin before we confess it—our confession accepts the sacrifice offered. "My little children, I am writing these things to you so that you may not sin. And if anyone sins, we have an Advocate with the Father, Jesus Christ the righteous; and He Himself is the propitiation for our sins; and not for ours only, but also for those of the whole world" (1 John 2:1, 2). The sin of the whole world was paid for at a single point in time. That means the price has been paid for those who love Jesus *and* for those who do not. Jesus became "the Lamb of God who takes away the sin of the world" (John 1:29). Again we are told that "God was in Christ reconciling the [whole] world to Himself" (2 Corinthians 5:19).

God's action independent of ours

God did not wait for us to repent from our sins. "But God demonstrates His own love toward us, in that while we were yet sinners, Christ died for us. Much more then, having now been justified by His blood, we shall be saved from the wrath of God through Him. For if while we were enemies we were reconciled to God through the death of His Son, much more, having been reconciled, we shall be saved by His life. And not only this, but we also exult in God through our Lord Jesus Christ, through whom we have now received the reconciliation" (Romans 5:8–11).

Jesus died for us while we were still sinners and God's enemies. God's love for us is not based on how we behave. He loves His children even though they have rebelled. From God's side, all have been saved. He loves us even if we don't respond. He paid the price to redeem us from sin. He waits with open arms, urging us to come home.

God's intention toward us

God does not desire that any human being die. "The Lord is not slow about His promise, as some count slowness, but is patient toward you, not wishing for any to perish but for all to come to repentance" (2 Peter 3:9). "This is good, and pleases God our Savior, who wants all people to be saved and to come to a knowledge of the truth" (1 Timothy 2:3, 4, NIV).

God first fused Himself to humanity through Jesus, combining God and man in one being. This is the perfect example of fusion. He lived a perfect life and ransomed all mankind, paying the once and forever price for our redemption. He reconciled us to the Father so we could live with Him forever. He defeated death and rose from the grave. "He chose us in Him before the foundation of the world, that we would be holy and blameless before Him. In love, He predestined us to adoption as sons through Jesus Christ to Himself, according to the kind intention of His will" (Ephesians 1:4–6).

The two Adams and solidarity

God describes what we receive through Adam: "Therefore, just as through one man sin entered into the world, and death through sin, . . . so death spread to all men, because all sinned" (Romans 5:12). Christ is the corporate head of mankind. This concept of solidarity translates into three essential points. First, in Adam God created all mankind (Acts 17:26). Second, Adam's separation from God placed all men in sin and under Satan's control. Detached from the source of life, they are destined to die. Third, God sent another corporate head in Jesus, Adam II, whose perfect life, death, and sacrifice brings for all mankind reconciliation to their separation from God (Romans 5:14).

Paul contrasts what we received from the first Adam and what we receive from Christ, the Second Adam. "For since by a man came death, by a man also came the resurrection of the dead. For as in Adam all die, so also in Christ all will be made alive. But each in his own order: Christ the first fruits, after that those who are Christ's at His coming" (1 Corinthians 15:21–23). We did not just receive the separated nature of sin; we have acted on our innate propensity to sin. We have committed sinful acts. We have neglected doing what we know to be right. We have failed to measure up to righteousness, and we have willfully rebelled against God. We have believed Satan's lies and distrusted God. We have acted on what we received from the first Adam and we have earned death. But in its place, Jesus offers us His life, His connection, and "eternal life" (Romans 6:23). How do we gain access to, or claim, what God has provided in this abundance of grace through the Second Adam?

"For if by the transgression of the one, death reigned through the one, much more *those who receive* the abundance of grace and of the gift of righteousness will reign in life through the One, Jesus Christ" (Romans 5:17; emphasis added). The corporate life of each Adam applies to us differently. Born under the first Adam, death is our automatic destiny. We must choose to receive a new corporate head by accepting Christ's sacrifice in exchange. Salvation only makes a difference "to those who receive."

"In Christ" we receive

"In Christ" we receive forgiveness. We get the forgiveness of sin not as an extended overture of God but as the consequence of being in Him. "In Him we have redemption through His blood, the forgiveness of our trespasses, according to the riches of His grace" (Ephesians 1:7). An exchange takes place as we accept Jesus as our corporate head: "He made Him who knew no sin to be sin on our behalf, so that we might become the righteousness of God in Him" (2 Corinthians 5:21). The trade doesn't seem fair from God's side—that He should take our sin and its penalty in order for us to have His life. It makes me think of the

old story *The Prince and the Pauper*, where doppelgangers trade places and experience each other's life. I, the pauper, step into His life as king.

"In Christ" we receive wisdom, righteousness, sanctification, and redemption. "But by His doing you are in Christ Jesus, who became to us *wisdom* from God, and *righteousness* and s*anctification*, and *redemption*, so that, just as it is written, 'LET HIM WHO BOASTS, BOAST IN THE LORD' " (1 Corinthians 1:30, 31; emphasis added). We have nothing to boast about. We must yield to God for Him to live in us so that His righteousness might shine through us. What is our part? We are invited to abide in Christ and to remain in Him (John 15:1–8).

"In Christ" we receive power. We have no power of our own; it is derived. We are like a sidecar for a motorcycle. Connected to God, we can do almost anything: "But thanks be to God, who gives us the victory through our Lord Jesus Christ" (1 Corinthian 15:57).

"In Christ" we join to Jesus' life. We are fused with all aspects of Christ's life, not just His past but His present life also. "God . . . even when we were dead in our transgressions, made us alive together with Christ (by grace you have been saved), and raised us up with Him, and seated us with Him in the heavenly places in Christ Jesus" (Ephesians 2:4–6). Jesus joins us to His own experience. He came, died, was resurrected, and was seated at the right hand of the Father. His past life becomes my history, His present my reality, His future my hope. At a point in history, God literally came to earth. He died, and every human being who finds salvation either looked forward to that event or looks back to His death, and through faith we enter Jesus' salvation history (Ephesians 2:8, 9).

"In Christ" we receive the right to become children of God. "But as many as received Him, to them He gave the right to become children of God, even to those who believe in His name, who were born, not of blood nor of the will of the flesh nor of the will of man, but of God" (John 1:12, 13). We don't become His children by being born into the right family. That is "not of blood." (You can imagine how that struck the Jews, who thought salvation was their birthright.) Not by the "will of the flesh," and not by human willpower. Not by self-help books, or counseling, or any other method of the "will of men" do we become His children. We are born as God's children—"of God" through His performance, not ours.

"In Christ" we receive completeness. We "are complete in Him" (Colossians 2:10, NKJV). We become complete when we fuse ourselves to Him. All the work has been completed; we simply need to access it.

"In Christ" we receive the sealing from the Holy Spirit. "In Him . . . you were sealed in Him with the Holy Spirit of promise, who is given as a pledge of our inheritance, with a view to the redemption of God's own possession, to the praise of His glory" (Ephesians 1:13, 14). Paul prays for the Holy Spirit to prepare the way for Jesus to dwell in us. "He would grant you, according to the riches of His glory, to be strengthened with power through His Spirit in the inner man, so that Christ may dwell in your hearts through faith" (Ephesians 3:16,17).

God's Holy Spirit connects us in this fusion process like a cord plugged into electricity or like a conduit for fueling a plane in flight. God attempts not only to make the initial connection but to keep the channel clear as He fuels us with life.

"In Christ" we receive salvation. "He made Him who knew no sin to be sin on our behalf, so that we might become the righteousness of God in Him" (2 Corinthians 5:21). "And there

is salvation in no one else" (Acts 4:12). The work that saves us, if indeed we can call it a work at all, is accepting Jesus Christ as our Lord. If we *have* Him, present tense, meaning if we currently enthrone Him on the control seat of our lives, then we have eternal life (1 John 5:12).

"In Christ" we receive a desire to respond. "Do you think lightly of the riches of His kindness . . . not knowing that the kindness of God leads you to repentance?" (Romans 2:4). To join with Him, we daily read His Word and meditate on it to seek His presence and purpose. We open our heart in prayer, speaking to Him as comfortably as we would a human friend yet bearing in our heart the recognition of His majesty. Our heart breaks out in worship, not just in songs of praise but in worship that inspires imitating our Lord and acting for Him. We crucify the old man, denying our sinful passions (Galatians 5:24). We die daily to the old nature (1 Corinthians 15:31). Seeking to have more of Him and less of us, we pick up His selfless nature and lay down our lives in service to others. While we desire our behavior to reflect His, eternal life comes not as a result of good behavior but as a result of living connected to Jesus as Lord of our life.

Ceremonies of fusion

Two ceremonies of the Christian church visually portray the truth that salvation consists of being joined with Christ. The first, baptism, not only signifies the washing away of sin but symbolizes uniting with Christ. Like a wedding ceremony, two individuals merge to become one new whole. I take on His name as a Christian: "Christ one." Christ's family becomes my family. I gain His sons and daughters as my brothers and sisters. All His assets become mine and all my debts His. He both adopts and marries me through this same ceremony (Galatians 3:27–29).

> Or do you not know that all of us who have been baptized into Christ Jesus have been baptized into His death? Therefore we have been buried with Him through baptism into death, so that as Christ was raised from the dead through the glory of the Father, so we too might walk in newness of life. For if we have become united with Him in the likeness of His death, certainly we shall also be in the likeness of His resurrection, knowing this, that our old self was crucified with Him, in order that our body of sin might be done away with, so that we would no longer be slaves to sin (Romans 6:3–6).

As the pastor lowers me into the water, the ceremony represents my fusion to Jesus' death. I die to sin, self, and my old lifestyle. Being immersed in water depicts dying to the old self and marks the closing of my former sinful life. When I rise up again out of the waters, I join with Christ's resurrection. His victory over sin and death becomes mine. An exchange takes place when I join to Him. He takes my sin, shame, and past life upon Himself, and He gives me all His righteousness as I renounce the former life. Only the form of baptism by immersion can represent these concepts of death, burial, and resurrection (Matthew 3:11; Mark 1:10; John 3:23). A baptism by sprinkling or pouring or rose petals misses the symbolism of being fused into Christ's experience.

The second fusion ceremony, Communion, represents a mini-baptism. Jesus took the

Passover meal, commemorating the substitute lamb and its blood, which allowed God to pass over the Israelites in judgment, and used it to point to His work to unite Himself with a sinful people (Mark 14:12; Luke 22:8; Exodus 12:13). At the meal, Jesus removed His outer garment and acted the part of a servant and washed His disciples' dirty feet. Peter vehemently refused to let His exalted Master perform this menial and humiliating task for him. He wanted to take care of his own dirty feet. But Jesus told Peter, "If I do not wash you, you have no part with Me" (John 13:8). This service represents accepting Christ's sacrifice. He must wash away my sin; I cannot do it myself. And in order to join with Him, I need to let Him clean me from the past life. Peter replied, "Lord, then wash not only my feet, but also my hands and my head" (John 13:9).

When Jesus rejoined the meal, He took up the unleavened bread and attached this emblem to His spotless life offered in place of ours. He lived the perfect life; Satan had nothing to claim Him. Unleavened bread became a fitting symbol for a sinless life! Taking in this bread at Communion means I fuse myself to the righteousness of Christ; it becomes mine. God can then pass over me in judgment because I have entered into Christ as my substitute. Righteousness is still His standard! Just as I cannot cleanse myself from sin, I do not have the perfect life to offer. So I join with Jesus' righteousness.

Jesus then picked up the cup. This unfermented grape juice represented a life poured out on my behalf. The Greek word used in Scripture for wine and grape juice is the same, *oinos*. Just as the unleavened bread has no taint of yeast, symbolizing a perfect and sinless life, the juice has no taint of fermentation, symbolizing Christ's sinless offering as well.

He declares, "This cup is the new covenant in My blood; do this, as often as you drink it, in remembrance of Me" (1 Corinthians 11:25). Jesus empowers the everlasting covenant by placing it in our hearts. This constitutes the new covenant in His blood. That covenant has always been, "I will be your God and you will be My people."

The juice symbolizes the means Christ uses to join me to His righteousness. Jesus gives up His life in order that we can have life. Jesus will wait to drink wine when He can live with us in physical reality. By drinking the unfermented juice, we acknowledge Jesus' sacrifice to give us His perfect life so we can commune with God.

This service represents our relationship with Christ. At my baptism and each time I enter into the communion service, I recommit to fusing my life to Jesus. I live with Him inside until I can see the God beyond my wildest dreams face-to-face.

Thoughts to Ponder

1. What does it mean to me to know that in Christ I am already sanctified? Have I emotionally accepted my standing with God?

_____

_____

_____

2. What does it mean that I am complete in Christ now? Can I accept that I am already complete in Him?

_____

_____

_____

3. When I was baptized, how much of the image of joining to Christ did I understand? When a couple joins in a wedding ceremony, how much do they fully understand of what the commitment means? Does that make the commitment any less real?

_____

_____

_____

4. What does it mean to me that God chose me and gave His life for me while I lived against Him? How does it give me hope when I sin or fail Him?

_____

_____

_____

5. How might I use the image of being marinated in Christ to explain to progressive Christians that Christ changes my life?

_____

_____

_____

_____

CHAPTER 6

The Family Mission Statement

"Can I live as a genuine Christian without joining or attending a church?" Yes, but like a soldier fighting alone, you decrease your impact. A tuba player might play without an orchestra, but don't expect the novelty to last long. God instructed His followers to stay together: "Let us . . . not [give] up meeting together, as some are in the habit of doing, but [let us encourage] one another—and all the more as you see the Day approaching" (Hebrews 10:25, NIV). God designed us as part of a mission-oriented spiritual community.

My family crafted its own mission statement as an extension of our values and purpose. The Berglund family mission is *to make Jesus the living center of our family, to build each other toward God's kingdom, to parade each other's strengths, to support each other in growing through our weaknesses, to openly express love and appreciation for each other, to never put each other down even to someone else, to have fun and enjoy life, to never stop loving, and to use our bond to reach the world for Jesus.* We haven't always lived our mission statement, but it helps to focus us in a specific direction.

The church forms God's family on earth with Him as the head. He also set specific goals so that His family would reflect Him and His values.

The pillar and foundation of truth

The church of the living God stands as the "pillar and foundation of the truth" (1 Timothy 3:15, NIV). In the Old Testament, God gave the church (the Israelites) in the wilderness "living words" of truth to pass along to the world (Acts 7:38, NIV). After years of His mercy, when the church at large continued to refuse truth from God, Jesus established a new church.

"Now when Jesus came into the district of Caesarea Philippi, He was asking His disciples saying, 'Who do people say that the Son of Man is?' And they said, 'Some say John the Baptist; and others, Elijah; but still others, Jeremiah, or one of the prophets.' He said to them, 'But who do you say that I am?' Simon Peter answered, 'You are the Christ, the Son of the Living God.' " Jesus declared that God Himself revealed this to him (Matthew 16:17).

Peter's willingness to accept new truth from God gave him the keys to the kingdom. "I also say to you that you are Peter, and upon this rock I will build My church; and the gates of Hades will not overpower it" (Matthew 16:18). Jesus used the Greek word *petra* when He said, "Upon this *rock* I will build My church." This feminine form for *rock* means "a large mass of rock, a ledge, or a shelf rock."

This chapter is based on Seventh-day Adventist fundamental beliefs no. 12, "The Church"; no. 13, "The Remnant and Its Mission"; and no. 14, "Unity in the Body of Christ."

Peter's name in the Greek is the masculine form *Petros*, meaning "the little rock." Jesus did not build the church upon Peter, "the little rock." Jesus built it on the truth that He is "the Christ, the Son of the living God." Peter acknowledged that Jesus was God, and Jesus founded the church on this rock-solid truth of salvation (Matthew 7:24).

The image of the rock points to Jesus (1 Corinthians 10:4). No one can lay a foundation other than Jesus. Scripture portrays Him as the capstone, the cornerstone, and the rock that sinners fall upon (1 Peter 2:4–8; Acts 4:8–12; Isaiah 28:16; Matthew 21:42; 1 Corinthians 3:11).

The church has the "key of knowledge" that the scribes and Pharisees sought to keep from the people (Luke 11:52). The knowledge of Christ's divinity and what He did on the cross unlocks salvation. Since Peter knew the truth of Jesus' identity and mission, he held the keys that would open salvation. Those who accept Jesus as God's sacrifice on our behalf become a part of the church.

Today people choose a church for a variety of reasons, including the musical program, the location, youth ministry, or the preacher's style. But the Bible tests a church by the truth it teaches. It also must lead individuals to connect with the person of Jesus and not just a doctrine (John 5:39, 40).

Many denominations compete for followers, but not all embrace the one true gospel (Galatians 1:6–9). The Bible specifies only "one Lord, one faith" (Ephesians 4:5). God has only one organized body as His visible church. Current culture teaches that we need tolerance, but true Christians oppose those teaching falsehood about God and spiritual things. God did not advocate religious pluralism. He called His disciples to separate themselves from the church of Israel. Christ Himself rejected the Jewish Church because it rejected truth about Him (Matthew 23:37–39).

The church visible

God has a visible body of believers to whom He has entrusted His truth. Early on, "The disciples were first called Christians in Antioch" (Acts 11:26) and at times were called members of "the way" (Acts 9:2; 19:9, 23; Galatians 1:13).

Jesus intentionally appointed twelve to carry His message and teachings and to have authority over demons (Mark 3:14–18). He called people to join the group by embracing the truth about Him as God (Matthew 28:18–20).

The term *church* (*ekklesia* in the Greek, meaning "a calling out"; and *qahal* in Hebrew, meaning "to congregate or assemble") points to a people visibly separated from the world. This visible church, even more prominent in the last days, preaches the gospel message to the entire world as a worldwide movement (Revelation 14:6). It comes on the scene after 1844, proclaiming the message—the judgment hour has begun (Revelation 14:6–17). This church keeps and promotes the observance of all the commandments of God, including the Sabbath command, and a call back to true worship (Revelation 14:12). God will bless His last-day church with the gift of prophecy as it holds its faith in Jesus (Revelation 12:17; 19:10). Its teaching will be in harmony with all of Scripture (Isaiah 8:20).

The Seventh-day Adventist Church fits this biblical description of the last-day church. Starting in the United States, it has exploded into a worldwide movement. Established after the beginning of the judgment in 1844, the Adventist Church's warning message, "The judgment hour has begun," bears relevance. This church teaches all of the commandments. God led this movement through a prophetic gift to grow from a handful of people to a church with a membership of more than nineteen million.

While God established a visible church, He has always had followers outside the visible body. "I have other sheep, which are not of this fold; I must bring them also, and they will hear My voice; and they will become one flock with one shepherd" (John 10:16).

The Holy Spirit lives in the hearts of Christians who belong to a vast array of denominations and some with no denomination at all. Living up to the full light they have now, they belong to Him. This group constitutes the church invisible. They will eventually join the fold and become "one flock" under one shepherd (John 10:16).

The church as body

God also uses the image of "the body" to describe His church. He pictures Himself as the head (Colossians 1:18). We become members of the body at our baptism (1 Corinthians 12:13). We receive spiritual gifts that help define our unique place as members in the body. Just as a hand has a role that the ear cannot fulfill, so God gives us unique gifts for a specific part of service.

Sometimes people say, "I don't believe in organized religion," and mentally I respond with, "Do you believe in disorganized religion?" I think they mean that they want freedom to function without being responsible to others or a codified belief. But a church, like a body, needs structure and organization to function. Imagine if each of your feet decided to travel in a different direction. This image of the church as a body helps me to understand the need for order and organization.

The organized church

Our Creator, a God of order, designed an organized church to represent Him to the world. The Old Testament church had organization. Moses set up the priesthood at God's command. Later, judges and supreme judges were set up (Deuteronomy 1:13–17). The church received commandments as a creed and followed very specific ceremonies. The temple served as a church building, and the tribes were organized under banners.

Later, in the New Testament, Jesus also formed an organized church. Even in His little band of twelve disciples He had a designated treasurer. The church in Acts held a common doctrinal belief (Acts 2:42); and the ability to sell property and distribute the proceeds necessitated a formally organized church (Acts 2:45). The church sent out chosen ministers to field assignments with letters of recommendation (Acts 11:22; 18:27).

The church recognized the God-given gifts to leaders called elders, or *presbuteros*, and overseers, or *episkopos*. The church also set aside deacons, or *diakonos*, to take care of the physical aspects of the church (Acts 6:1–3). Paul admonished fellow believers to submit to these appointed leaders(1 Thessalonians 5:12).

While the gifts we receive equip us for specific ministry for God, some areas of ministry remain essential for all believers. For instance, God expects all of us to proclaim the gospel and minister to others on His behalf (1 Peter 2:9).

The authoritative church

The church derives its authority from Christ, the Incarnate Word, and from Scripture, the Written Word. While God calls each individual to scriptural accountability, the collective voice of all of the members through representation at a denomination-wide meeting forms the voice of the church. When some questioned Paul and Barnabas's theology and practice, the men appealed to the central church body. "When they arrived at Jerusalem, they were received by the church and the apostles and the elders, and they reported all that God had done with them" (Acts 15:4).

The council, consisting of the elders, leaders, and the "whole church," ruled and then issued an official decree. A local church must listen to the council of the sisterhood of churches. Wisdom is found in a multitude of councillors. A group of believers keep us from being tossed back and forth with "every wind of doctrine" and allows us to stay balanced and accountable (Ephesians 4:14).

God leads His church even if she refuses to follow. Joshua and Caleb stood for truth when the congregation in the wilderness voted against God (Numbers 14:5–9). God did not separate them from the church even when it went into the wilderness for forty years. Even when the church does not make the right decisions, we need not separate ourselves from it unless it ceases to be the church of God. Speak your convictions at the proper time, and then wait for God to act. After a generation passed, God led His church, with Joshua and Caleb, into the Promised Land (Numbers 14:24).

We can accomplish much more while united than we can individually. The Seventh-day Adventist worldwide church structure makes it possible to operate the largest Protestant educational and health-care systems in the world, hold satellite evangelism, own youth camps, conduct global television and radio ministries, mobilize for disaster relief, minister to and develop impoverished areas, and manage one of the largest Protestant publishing systems in the world. We should praise God for this plan.

The church as the temple of God

God uses the temple building as a portal to His presence. This illustrates the purpose of the church. God lives by His Spirit in the midst of His church, and His people become His dwelling place. God adds us like living stones to the building (1 Peter 2:4–6). Lifting Christ before the people, calling them to worship, and inviting them to enthrone Christ become our goals.

Even in the midst of corruption, Christ made it His practice to go to the church because He could still meet God in His temple (Luke 4:16). We should not exclude ourselves from church because unholy people go there. People don't make the church holy; the Lord's presence makes it holy. Whether the preacher preaches well or the singers sing on key, God is still God—present with His people, the church, as they assemble each Sabbath.

Many today argue about the place we worship or the form of our worship. While Scripture does give some principles that can help, no specific order of worship has been given in Scripture. But God emphasizes the uncompromising need for heart worship (John 4:21–24).

The church as family

How will people know if they have become a part of God's family? "By this all men will know that you are My disciples, if you have love for one another" (John 13:35). God uses the church to support each believer with love (Ephesians 3:15–21). He lives as our Father (Galatians 4:6). He adopts us as His children (Romans 8:14–16; 1 John 3:1). If we love God as our Father, we should love His children as our brothers and sisters (1 John 5:1). We will sustain each other in fellowship (Philippians 1:1–4).

God admonishes church members to care for each other like the ideal family. God intended the church to supply an environment where people can grow. For the members of the church to love each other, we must live with grace, mercy, accountability, respect, and deep loyalty. We come from different socioeconomic, cultural, and political backgrounds, but the love of God unifies us in our diversity. For us as a family, passing our common religious values to our children becomes a chief goal.

God made provision to keep His family together. He outlines the responsibility we have to resolve conflict (Matthew 18:15–17), and God instructs us in an appropriate process for handling a private offense (Galatians 6:1). If the erring member rejects the wisdom and authority of the church, he severs himself from its fellowship.

As with any family, our relationships sometimes need restoration, which should always be the purpose of church discipline. Though "all have sinned and fall short of the glory of God," flagrant rebellion or continued offenses that bring reproach on the church should be dealt with by censure or disfellowshiping the offender (Romans 3:23, NIV; 1 Corinthians 5:4–13). Disfellowshiping removes the evil that could influence others and acts as a redemptive remedy for the offender. Treating them as nonbelievers, members should do all in their power to reeducate them, encourage them, and restore their relationship with Christ and His church (2 Corinthians 2:6–10).

The mission

Who does the church war against? "For our struggle is not against flesh and blood, but against the rulers, against the powers, against the world forces of this darkness, against the spiritual forces of wickedness in the heavenly places" (Ephesians 6:12).

The church stands as a fortress against Satan—and we must go on the offensive. We war against Satan by proclaiming the gospel to a dying world. Not just for the purpose of informing them but for the sake of transforming them into the image of God (Matthew 28:16–20).

By understanding the church's family mission statement, we can get a glimpse of the Father who formed it. The church must not forget that its mission is to bring all to a saving knowledge and relationship with Jesus. This picture represents a relational, merciful, compassionate God intent on bringing us back to Him—a God beyond our wildest dreams.

Thoughts to Ponder

1. Meet together with your family and create your own family mission statement. Elements might include how you will treat each other, what you will do to reach the community, and your commitment to keep God at the center.

2. The church is compared to a body with different parts carrying on different functions. What is my function in the church?

3. Have I looked at my vocation as a calling from God to ministry? How might I use it more for the kingdom?

4. How do I relate to church authority? Do I show respect for the positions in which God has placed people?

5. Have I extended myself to others in the church to support them in their walk as Christians? Do I have people who mentor me like Paul or people I mentor like Timothy? How can I encourage others?

CHAPTER 7

The Creator's Gift to Me

Have you ever searched for the perfect gift for that special someone? Aftershave seems so impersonal. The beauty of cut flowers soon fades. A silver candle snuff may be elegant but all too impractical. You want the Swiss Army knife of gifts. You need something that expresses the love, hope, and dreams you share and that also reminds the person of you and your commitment to him or her. Ideally, the gift would meet a real need. The Creator designed the Sabbath day as the perfect gift for us.

The sign He is my Creator

The Sabbath gift identifies God both as *the* Creator and *my personal* Creator. The creation story in the original Hebrew employs an "envelope construction," enclosing corresponding statements with opening and closing capping sections that echo each other. In this Genesis account, the envelope construction uses the seventh-day Sabbath as a signature that God created in seven literal days. The Creator intricately weaves the Sabbath into the signature of His work. The envelope construction has each day formed and then filled to complement what was formed.

Formed: **God Created**

God Formed	*God Filled*
Day 1: Light	Day 4: Sun, Moon, Stars
Day 2: Air/Water	Day 5: Fowl, Fish
Day 3: Land	Day 6: Animals, Man

Filled Day 7: **The Sabbath Day**

In contemporary language, God tagged the day as His "Creator day" so everyone would realize that the day belongs to Him. This established a weekly cycle. Unlike other time measurements—a day, a month, or a year—it does not depend on the movement of sun, moon, or stars. The weekly cycle, closing on the Sabbath, testifies of a Creator.

God acts on the first Sabbath. "By the seventh day God completed His work which He had done, and He rested on the seventh day from all His work which He had done. Then God blessed the seventh day and sanctified it, because in it He rested from all His work which God had created and made" (Genesis 2:2, 3). The reference to "the seventh day" identifies a specific day. God did not say He would honor one day out of every seven days but He selected the seventh-day Sabbath.

This chapter is based on Seventh-day Adventist fundamental beliefs no. 6, "Creation"; and no. 20, "The Sabbath."

God "blessed" this specific day, and He *sanctified* it, setting it apart with His holy presence. He "rested" from His work, not only setting an example for humans but spending time with them.

God's gift meant the giving of Himself to humankind. The word used for "sanctified it" in the Hebrew is *qadash*, which means "to make holy." God made the day holy the same way He made the ground holy before Moses, the same way He made the sanctuary holy, the same way He makes His people holy—by placing His presence there in a unique way (Exodus 3:5; 1 Corinthians 1:2). We don't choose the day—God does. God offered access to Himself in a special way through this day so that we could commune with Him as our personal Creator.

The sign that He is my Provider

The Sabbath gift assures me that I can trust God to be my Provider. With Israel's enslavement, God's people were exposed to the Egyptians praying, worshiping, and sacrificing to false gods to meet their daily needs. In response, God established Himself as their one and only Creator and set Himself apart from the worship of the created things they had deified. God gave them manna to test them and to teach them to rely on Him and to instill the importance of the Sabbath (Exodus 16:4, 5). He performed a threefold miracle to show He was not just their Creator but also their Provider. First, twice the amount of bread came down Friday, the sixth day. Second, God preserved it overnight. Third, God did not send manna on the day we now call Saturday, the seventh day. God used His signature day, the Sabbath, to sign the gift of manna so His people would know it came from Him.

He also showed that Friday (the sixth day) is the day of preparation in order to get ready to meet God on the Sabbath (Exodus 16:23, 24). By performing their routine chores ahead of time, the Israelites would have the Sabbath to focus on their time with God.

The sign to worship Him

The Sabbath gift gives me opportunity to worship God as my Creator. When I acknowledge God as my Creator, I place myself in the position of a subordinate as His creature. "Remember the sabbath day, to keep it holy. Six days you shall labor and do all your work, but the seventh day is a sabbath of the LORD your God; in it you shall not do any work, you or your son or your daughter, your male or your female servant or your cattle or your sojourner who stays with you. For in six days the LORD made the heavens and the earth, the sea and all that is in them, and rested on the seventh day; therefore the Lord blessed the sabbath day and made it holy" (Exodus 20:8–11).

An attitude of remembrance can be a gift. If we continue to remember God as Creator, we will see ourselves as His creatures. Seeing His worth above ours inspires true worship—in fact, *worship*'s original etymology breaks down to "worth-ship."

In one sense, the seventh-day Sabbath carries the significance of a wedding ring. When we observe it, we share with the world our commitment to God—that He claims us as His bride. Could you imagine your fiancé giving you a wedding ring and you responding that you would prefer to get your own ring? This day came to us as an intimate wedding gift from the Bridegroom.

We join with all humanity in acknowledging ourselves as creatures before our Creator. Sons, daughters, servants, and strangers join together as fellow creatures worshiping the same Creator. Truly observing the Sabbath would break down prejudice, racism, and class distinction.

The sign He is my Deliverer

Observing the Sabbath gift memorializes God as my Deliverer. The book of Deuteronomy also gives its own account of the Ten Commandments. Here, the purpose for the Sabbath command reads, "Observe the sabbath day to keep it holy. . . . You shall remember that you were a slave in the land of Egypt, and the LORD your God brought you out of there by a mighty hand and by an outstretched arm; therefore the LORD your God commanded you to observe the sabbath day" (Deuteronomy 5:12–15). Deuteronomy adds an additional reason for keeping the Sabbath: not only should we honor God as Creator but also as Deliverer.

The Sabbath reminded Israel that before God brought deliverance, they were slaves. Their predicament should resonate with us because before Christ redeemed us, we served Satan as slaves. The Sabbath foreshadowed Jesus hanging on the cross so I could walk free. His death would bring us freedom from the bondage of Satan. God introduced deliverance as a reason for Sabbath observance clear back in Moses' day. Because Jesus delivered us from the bondage of Satan and rested on the Sabbath day as a sign of its completion, we see that God intended deliverance to be a foundational concept portrayed by the Sabbath day from its inception.

The sign of the covenant

The Sabbath gift offers everyone an opportunity to enter into His covenant. " 'How blessed is the man who does this . . . who keeps from profaning the sabbath, and keeps his hand from doing any evil.' Let not the foreigner who has joined himself to the LORD say, 'The LORD will surely separate me from His people.' . . . Even those I will bring to My holy mountain and make them joyful in My house of prayer. Their burnt offerings and their sacrifices will be acceptable on My altar; for My house will be called a house of prayer for all the peoples" (Isaiah 56:2, 3, 7).

Even in the Old Testament, the Sabbath extended beyond the Jews. This passage promises its blessing to the "man" who keeps from profaning the Sabbath, not to the "Jew" who keeps from profaning the Sabbath. In fact, this whole passage explicitly states that the Sabbath was intended to be a sign to anyone who wants to accept God. God established the Sabbath in Eden before the Jewish nation existed (Genesis 2:2, 3). God commanded that the Jews give everyone within their circle of influence, slaves and foreigners alike, the Sabbath off so they too could worship.

Jesus would later specify that the purpose of creating the Sabbath was to benefit all of mankind (Mark 2:27). God does not refer to the Sabbath day as the "Jewish day" but as "My holy day" or "the holy day of the LORD" (Isaiah 58:13; Exodus 20:8).

Beyond extending this day to the Gentiles in general, this passage extends the day to the marginalized. To those who repent and seek Him, God gave the Sabbath as a sign of joining His covenant people. They accepted Yahweh as their God and confirmed the offer for God to take them as His people. God signed an open adoption offer in the Sabbath for any who might choose to become a part of His family. And He announced that His house will be a house of prayer for *all* people.

The sign of surrender

The Sabbath gift symbolically portrays dying to self and living by faith. "If because of the sabbath, you turn your foot from doing your own pleasure on My holy day, and call the sabbath a delight, the holy day of the LORD honorable, and honor it, desisting from your own ways, from seeking your own pleasure and speaking your own word, then you will take delight in the LORD, and I will make you ride on the heights of the earth; and I will feed you with the heritage of Jacob your father, for the mouth of the LORD has spoken" (Isaiah 58:13, 14). Those who view the Sabbath as a painful obligation miss the true delight promised for celebrating the Sabbath with a heart tuned toward God. God desires to give us a day free from work and selfish, superficial pleasures so that we can "take delight in the Lord."

God promises in this passage to grant those who observe His Sabbath the heritage of Jacob. God changed Jacob's name to Israel, making his heirs children of God. Their blessing as God's children included holiness of character (Deuteronomy 4:7; 28:1; Leviticus 19:2), health (Exodus 15:26; Deuteronomy 7:13), superiority of craftsmanship (Exodus 31:2–6), material prosperity (Deuteronomy 8:17, 18), and national greatness (Deuteronomy 4:6–8).

The sign He makes me holy

When I accept His Sabbath gift, I confess that the Lord makes me holy. "Also I gave them My sabbaths to be a sign between Me and them, that they might know that I am the LORD who sanctifies them" (Ezekiel 20:12). The Sabbath symbolizes that I recognize that He makes me holy. He functions as my Re-creator as well as my Creator. After Jesus lived the perfect human life, He laid Himself down in sacrifice, proclaiming, "It is finished," and we have nothing to add (John 19:30).

Some Christians accuse Sabbath keepers of being legalists, but when we observe the Sabbath we declare Jesus as our source of holiness (Ezekiel 20:20). To ignore the day that He has set aside constitutes spiritual treason. Keeping the Sabbath enthrones Him as Lord. Obeying crowns Him Lord of our lives.

The sign that He recreates me

Observing the Sabbath gift acknowledges God's role as our Re-creator. After Jesus' crucifixion they took His body down, wrapped it in linen, and laid Him in the tomb. "It was the preparation day, and the Sabbath was about to begin. Now the women who had come with Him out of Galilee followed, and saw the tomb and how His body was laid. Then they returned and prepared spices and perfumes. And on the Sabbath they rested according to the commandment" (Luke 23:54–56).

Jesus declared, "It is finished," and in His death He laid His perfect life to our account. The bondage of Satan is broken. Just as He rested after accomplishing creation, He now rests after accomplishing re-creation. When we rest on the Sabbath, we observe a day that calls to our memory the sacrifice Jesus provided for us in leaving heaven, joining with humanity, living the perfect life, and offering it sacrificially for us.

The disciples observed the Sabbath at the time of Jesus' death. Evidently nothing that Jesus said during His entire earthly ministry gave them any thought that the Sabbath observance was changed, or that it had become unimportant; neither do they indicate any doubt as to which day to observe as the Sabbath. This seventh-day Sabbath has been kept in an unbroken line by Jews and Christians alike up to the present day. There are more than nineteen million Christian Sabbath keepers who honor the hours between sundown on Friday night and sundown on Saturday night as the Sabbath. They observe the day not as a mere duty but as a joy that they enter a deeper relationship with Him on that day. God tells us, "If you love Me, you will keep My commandments" (John 14:15).

The sign I follow Jesus
Embracing the Sabbath gift follows Jesus' example. "And He came to Nazareth, where He had been brought up; and as was His custom, He entered the synagogue on the Sabbath" (Luke 4:16). Jesus went to church regularly on Saturday, the seventh-day Sabbath. In fact, Jesus claimed to be "Lord of the Sabbath" (Luke 6:5). He performed the work of His Father, He healed and restored lives on that day, and He declared it "lawful to do good on the Sabbath" (Matthew 12:12). Jesus corrected the Pharisees' misunderstanding of the Sabbath day as a set of rules, but He never changed the day. He pointed again to its value for ministering to people, but He never abolished it as God's holy day.

He came to fill the Sabbath full of meaning. "Do not think that I came to abolish the Law or the Prophets; I did not come to abolish but to fulfill. For truly I say to you, until heaven and earth pass away, not the smallest letter or stroke shall pass from the Law until all is accomplished. Whoever then annuls one of the least of these commandments, and teaches others to do the same, shall be called least in the kingdom of heaven; but whoever keeps and teaches them, he shall be called great in the kingdom of heaven" (Matthew 5:17–19).

They had missed the deep significance of God's law. He revealed that He based the commandment "you shall not murder" on the concept of not hating (Matthew 5:21, 22). Not committing adultery included turning one's heart away from lust (Matthew 5:27, 28). The deeper significance did not void the law; it only enhanced or amplified it. In the same way, Jesus pointed to the heart experience of the Sabbath. Placing God as Lord of my heart does not nullify the specifics of the commandment.

Jesus kept the day Himself, His disciples kept it after His death, and He believed that they would be keeping it when Titus destroyed the temple in A.D. 70. He said, "But pray that your flight will not be in the winter, or on a Sabbath" (Matthew 24:20). We certainly can understand why winter would be a hardship as they fled from Jerusalem. But He would only have told them to pray that their flight not be on the Sabbath if the Sabbath day were still going to be in effect some forty years after His death.

His disciples also followed after their Master in observing the seventh-day Sabbath. "And according to Paul's custom, he went to them, and for three Sabbaths reasoned with them from the Scriptures" (Acts 17:2). This mentions Paul's Sabbath church attendance and states that it was his custom.

The sign of resting in salvation

Observing the Sabbath day, we enter into the rest of salvation in Jesus. "For He has spoken in a certain place of the seventh day in this way: 'And God rested on the seventh day from all His works' " (Hebrews 4:4, NKJV). "So there remains a Sabbath rest for the people of God. For the one who has entered His rest has himself also rested from his works, as God did from His" (Hebrews 4:9, 10). The author of Hebrews mourns the fact that in the past, God's followers didn't enter into the rest of salvation that comes by faith in Jesus Christ because of their unbelief. Then the author compares the rest of salvation in Jesus to the rest of the Sabbath and mentions there remains a *Sabbath rest*. The seventh-day Sabbath represents the rest from working on our own power. It demonstrates believing in the all-sufficient sacrifice of Jesus Christ. We do not keep the Sabbath to be saved, but rather we keep it in joyful recognition that God has saved us.

The Sabbath connects me in worship to my Creator; it gives me trust in my Provider, and it reminds me that He delivers me and makes me holy. I rest in it as He did on this earth and in re-creation. And in it I find the God beyond my wildest dreams.

Thoughts to Ponder

1. The Sabbath was given as a sign with many facets. What facet do I normally associate with the Sabbath? What facet covered here was most unique to me?

_____

_____

_____

2. What does the Sabbath tell me about God and His desire to have a relationship with me? What does it tell me about who He is?

_____

_____

_____

3. What benefit might it be to share my understanding of the Sabbath with Christians of another faith? What could I share with someone who was shy about letting others know they keep the Sabbath and encourage them to be open about their Sabbath observance?

_____

_____

_____

4. Where do I find myself devaluing the Sabbath? What might I change to help make the Sabbath more significant for myself and my family?

_____

_____

_____

5. What can I do to make the Sabbath more than a commandment to be observed? How can it be a personal encounter with Jesus for myself and my family?

_____

_____

_____

CHAPTER 8

Family as It Was Meant to Be

A young businesswoman was approached by a real estate agent who wanted to sell her a home. "A home?" she said. "Why do I need a home? I was born in a hospital, educated in a boarding school, courted in an automobile, and married in a church. My husband and I work in office buildings. On weekends, we spend our mornings playing golf and our afternoons playing bridge at the club. Evenings we go to the movies. And when I die I'm going to be buried from a funeral parlor. I don't need a home, all I need is a garage!"[1]

My family

I need to share my belief concerning family. Besides God, my family has brought me the greatest joy in my life. Scenes play through my mind like snapshots in a photo album. My dad out in the yard squirting my brothers and me with the water hose on a hot summer day, and then Mom opening the door with a pitcher of ice-cold water and pouring it over my dad's head—and quickly retreating into the house. Then Dad, undaunted, kinking the hose and running after her into the house, and then laughter and water exploding everywhere.

My family wasn't perfect. We faced significant financial hardship. All of us had our own individual struggles. Some dealt with the grind of life; others fought insecurities, weaknesses, or addictions. With four testosterone-filled boys, there were even occasional physical fights between us. But at the end of the day we recognized that we could fail and struggle and sometimes behave poorly but still find understanding, love, and belonging.

God created the family

God designed the human family to be different from animal families. Compare how human children develop in contrast to the young of other animals. Gray foxes are left to make their own way at about nine months, and harp seals leave their young after about twelve days of nurturing. But human kids rarely leave home until their late teens or early twenties. Human babies depend on parents to nurture and care for them.

Why did God create human babies so dependent? I think it has to do with His design of the family. Meeting the child's need increases the parental bond and the influence on the child. God intended the family to serve as the vehicle to transfer values, instill socialization, and train for survival. God created the family as a place to learn of Him and experience His gracious love and mercy.

I feel for those who are recovering from the brokenness of a dysfunctional family. In

This chapter is based on Seventh-day Adventist fundamental belief no. 23, "Marriage and the Family."

these families, conflict, abuse, and neglect lead members to learn coping styles to survive. Mental illnesses, substance abuse, or addictions can go untreated and create an unhealthy environment for children or spouses to thrive and grow. Unfortunately, some families seem to struggle with each other instead of supporting each other.

Marriage: The cornerstone for family

God built the foundation of the family on marriage in the Garden of Eden. "Then the Lord God said, 'It is not good for the man to be alone; I will make him a helper suitable for him' " (Genesis 2:18). "For this reason a man shall leave his father and his mother, and be joined to his wife; and they shall become one flesh" (Genesis 2:24). He created a helpmate for Adam. There are two Hebrew words that make up the meaning for helper or helpmate. The first comes from the Hebrew word *ezer*. Originally, this word carried the meaning "to save" or "to be strength"; at times it is translated "savior." The second word, *k'enegdo*, means one "exactly corresponding to" or "a complement." God formed a perfect complement for Adam to strengthen him, and to make him whole.

Reflection of God

"Then God said, 'Let Us make man in Our image, according to Our likeness;' . . . God created man in His own image, in the image of God He created him; male and female He created them" (Genesis 1:26, 27). God created mankind after His image. He says He created mankind as male and female, and they mirror His image as they marry and become one. Thus the two become one whole flesh. Male and female were created from God's hand as complements, not as superior and inferior. Though not identical, they function in cooperation and deference to each other.

Other unions fail to portray the image of complements formed and coming together to represent the divine union. Two males joining together, two females joining together, or multiple people joining in a marriage, do not fulfill God's intention. They are not mutual complements designed uniquely to join together to form the whole. Physically, men and women were made to fit together; they form reproductive opposites. From their first union, God would multiply and fill the earth. They would do that as an outgrowth of the full love they felt for each other expressed in the two coming together in the intimacy of knowing each other. "So they are no longer two, but one flesh. What therefore God has joined together, let no man separate" (Matthew 19:6).

Each parent has a unique role after the birth of a child. Only women can nurse children at their breast. Children have a natural role model in the parent of the same sex; and by observing a mother's and father's relationship, children may learn how to relate to the opposite sex.

Marriage: A three-strand cord

The covenant promise of marriage binds the couple together with God as long as they both shall live (Romans 7:2, 3). Christian marriage forms a three-cord strand between a man, a woman, and God that shall not be broken (Ecclesiastes 4:12). They pledge themselves to each other before God. He enters into the relationship and supplies a divine love that they in turn share with each other. Marriage becomes the place where God showcases His unconditional love through forgiveness, mercy, and resilient love. The God-filled spouse becomes the human ambassador to minister love to His child. God intended our spouse to support us toward heaven and to strengthen our relationship with Him.

Unequally yoked marriages miss God's purpose

God purposes to use marriage to bring His children home. Because of that, He counsels, "Do not be bound together with unbelievers; for what partnership have righteousness and lawlessness, or what fellowship has light with darkness?" (2 Corinthians 6:14). God knows the values of a believer and a nonbeliever will set them at odds. For the unbeliever, self-serving is all important; this hinders marriage and family relationships. While there are exceptions, rarely does a believer marry and then convert an unbelieving spouse.

I have counseled many unequally yoked marriages in trouble after a Christian loved a nonbeliever, married, and then the couple found they were in conflict as one tried to live a dedicated Christian life. They clash on observing Sabbath, paying tithe, giving offerings, raising children, believing in Christian education, serving in ministry, worshiping in the family, attending Christian summer camp, attending church, and praying.

Overwhelmingly, couples who try to mix their religions find that their own house is divided against itself. Christian and non-Christian goals place them on different sides of the field, and the parents find themselves competing rather than cooperating because they head in opposite directions.

Sex: A blessing

Cleaving means being welded, or soldered, together. In the marriage ceremony, the couple pledges themselves exclusively to each other. God created humans as sexual beings. The act of sexual intimacy transcends the joining of two bodies; it represents the uniting of two individuals at the deepest level. By this act, they become vulnerable. The physical act expresses the ultimate of sharing all that they have—material possessions, feelings, thoughts, hopes, fears, successes, and failures. For this reason, God condemns sex outside of marriage. Many consenting young adults excuse premarital sex as a victimless crime, but the act of sex is a promise that they are giving themselves fully and forever to each other—it has a psychologically binding effect.

Polygamy, fornication (sex outside of marriage), homosexuality, bestiality, and adultery fail to fit into God's plan because they do not express commitment. God identifies them as sin because selfishness, not love, motivates them (Exodus 20:14; Leviticus 20:10–12; Proverbs 6:24–32; 1 Corinthians 6:9, 13, 18; Galatians 5:19; Ephesians 5:3; 1 Thessalonians 4:3). Instead of saving myself for a spouse within a marriage commitment, I grab at these to pleasure myself. God did not create us like animals, driven by our hormones and selfish, base passions. He granted us the ability to choose to put another person's needs above our own, above our natural inclination. To achieve this, He created the gift of sex within a committed marriage. Godly sexuality involves the giving of myself to the "complement" God gave me in order to meet the other person's needs and pleasure.

Children: The little fruits of love

Children are intended to be a natural by-product of the love between a husband and wife. A child lives as a blend of both mother and father. Children are meant to be a blessing. "Like arrows in the hand of a warrior, so are the children of one's youth" (Psalm 127:4). In an agrarian society, having a "quiver full of them" translated into financial blessing (Psalm 127:5). Children in contemporary society, though more of a financial drain, provide an emotional blessing. They give us someone for whom to care, because love needs an object.

Training children

God has entrusted children's character development to their parents. The home is the first school, where parents teach, train, empower, and support their children. This early teaching removes the children's sense of entitlement, prepares them for service to humanity, instills spiritual values in them, and connects them with God. God instructs parents to "teach [the love of the Lord] diligently to your sons and . . . talk of [this love] when you sit in your house and when you walk by the way and when you lie down and when you rise up" (Deuteronomy 6:7). The Bible says, "Train up a child in the way he should go, even when he is old he will not depart from it" (Proverbs 22:6). That does not mean they cannot reject it; it means they will not be able to escape the truth that has been planted in their hearts.

Divorce

God offers us a vision of family that starts on the foundation of a committed, loving marriage. Unfortunately, many find themselves in a less-than-ideal marriage. No marriage is so dead that God cannot resurrect it if both parties are willing. Transformed by the power of God, each partner can become a new creature. From that point on, they enter a new marriage because one or both of them have radically changed.

When a marriage has two sinful human beings, one or both can back out of their commitment. It only takes one to destroy the relationship. Both parties often have a part in the demise of a marriage, but one party can victimize a completely innocent spouse. One partner can break the marriage through addiction, sexual exploits, drug or alcohol abuse, or mental illness, and the other partner can feel powerless to hold the marriage together. Try as one might, a person cannot force another to act civilly, rationally, lovingly, or honorably.

In Malachi, God clearly expresses His view of divorce: " 'I hate divorce,' says the Lord" (2:16). Should we expect anything less from a God who loves us? What father would not ache for his child going through a divorce? In God's case, *both* children involved belong to Him. Who wouldn't hate a choice that causes children to suffer as innocent victims?

God hates divorce because it shatters a relationship meant to convey and portray His unconditional love not only to the spouses and children but also to the onlooking world. "What therefore God has joined together, let not man separate" (Matthew 19:6, ESV). God intended for marriages not to be dissolved. When He called for a certificate of divorce to be given when couples decided to divorce, He wasn't condoning the divorce but protecting the woman in a divorce. Jesus said that this provision was made because of the hardness of their hearts (Matthew 19:8). One or both parties would not let God give them love. A "certificate of divorce" made the husband surrender his claim on the wife's dowry. Literally, it means that if you are set on divorce, at least make human provision for the need of the one you promised to take care of for life.

God hates divorce but loves divorcées. He wraps His arms around each of His children and grieves with them in their loss. He welcomes them to His healing love with open arms. Some, He assures through His Spirit, have done all possible to restore their relationship from their side. They should not feel guilt; they have done their part. The general community may have no idea what they have been through. They may not know the extenuating circumstances that have caused the divorce. The victims of divorce should not be shunned in church society. The church should be an extension of God's open arms. We should love and support each person struggling through a divorce.

With so many divorces—and Christian marriages having almost the same divorce rate as the rest of the population—it seems as if marriage is a high-risk gamble. Genuine Christian marriages may have a great advantage. Most statistics are based on those who claim Christianity, not on those who live Christianity. Phillip C. McGraw writes in his best-selling book *Relationship Rescue*, "The reported divorce rate among couples that pray together is about one in ten thousand."[2] Clearly, "except the LORD build the house, they labour in vain that build it" (Psalm 127:1, KJV).

The great family expectation

God intended the family to give us a little taste of heaven on earth. He wanted us to experience His love. "We know love by this, that He laid down His life for us; and we ought to lay down our lives for the brethren" (1 John 3:16).

Years passed, and we became empty nesters. I have heard people say how wonderful and free they felt without their kids. I feel like I lost one of my arms. It hasn't ended my life, but it has changed so much of my normal day-to-day functioning. I would not stop my children from pursuing God's calling in their lives or stunt their independence, but I love our family; I love living together and sharing together. I am as proud of them as a father can be, and I raised them to be strong, responsible, and independent.

I have seen extended families that still live intertwined, offering each other support and encouragement in one place. For now, my own family lives scattered across America, and I fight distance and time to keep up on each of their daily lives. I live for the day when I can laugh, learn, grow, and live together as a giant family with God as our Father. The God who planned the idea of family is the God beyond my wildest dreams.

---

1. Barry Emondson, "Only Jesus Can Make a House a Home," *Sermon Central*, accessed June 29, 2016, http://www.sermoncentral.com/sermons/only-jesus-can-make-a-house-a-home-barry-edmondson-sermon-on-weddings-113882.

2. Phillip C. McGraw, *Relationship Rescue: A Seven-Step Strategy for Reconnecting With Your Partner* (New York: Hachette, 2001), 292.

Thoughts to Ponder

1. What things make my family unique? How has my family progressed in understanding and supporting each other?

_____

_____

_____

2. What are my responsibilities to my family? (See 1 Timothy 5:8.) Emotionally? Spiritually? Socially? Physically? Financially?

_____

_____

_____

3. How can I support families who are struggling through divorce?

_____

_____

_____

4. Who in my family do I have the hardest time loving? How do I deal with the dysfunctions in my family?

_____

_____

_____

5. Do I have a family devotional time? What steps do I need to take to help establish that in my family?

_____

_____

_____

CHAPTER 9

Principles to Live By

When I became a Christian, I announced that Jesus now lives in me as my Lord. I desired with Paul to crucify self so that "I no longer live, but Christ lives in me" (Galatians 2:20, NIV). I wanted, and still want, everything I say, do, watch, play, eat, or drink to glorify God (1 Corinthians 10:31). In the beginning of my Christian walk, I used the Ten Commandments as a rule book to gain salvation. I later learned that God gave the commandments to Israel, saying, "I am the LORD your God, who brought you out of the land of Egypt, out of the house of slavery" (Exodus 20:2). God gave the commands to a people He had already *claimed* and *delivered* to show them what it looked like to live as His children. Now that they were His people, He sought to live inside of them.

The commandments are love codified. The first four commandments show me how to love God, and the last six how to love humans (Exodus 20:1–17; Matthew 22:36–40). When He gave these commandments, which demonstrate a love far beyond their human capabilities, their honest response should have been to cry out with Paul, "Wretched man that I am! Who will set me free from the body of this death?" (Romans 7:24). Their answer and ours should echo the words of Paul: "Thanks be to God through Jesus Christ our Lord!" (Romans 7:25).

Initially, I tried to keep the law, and then I realized that I couldn't live out these commands on my own, so I invited Jesus to live through me. The sanctuary system, given with the law, showed how God would deal with sin through Jesus. I want to live out these precepts in order to glorify God and allow others to see His selfless character of love in me.

In order to surrender my life to Him and His cause, I seek to live between two extremes. I must not let rule-keeping become my means of salvation. I want to respond to Jesus relationally, not out of mere duty. If I trust my performance to make me right with God, I have lost sight of grace. I fool myself if I buy into the belief that I can earn my way to heaven (Galatians 5:4). Neither can I ignore that a Christian behaves differently than a non-Christian. I boast freedom in Christ, but I must not let that freedom be an excuse to sin (Galatians 5:13). As much as I need to guard myself against legalism, I also need to guard myself against liberal rationalization. I cannot trust my natural, sin-tainted inclination. "There is a way which seems right to a man, but its end is the way of death" (Proverbs 14:12). I cannot let the things of the world crowd out Jesus (Matthew 13:22).

Even good things can become like excessive weights if they divert me from worshiping and living for Him (Hebrews 12:1, 2). Christ must be first in my life; then He will supply

This chapter is based on Seventh-day Adventist fundamental beliefs no. 19, "The Law of God"; and no. 22, "Christian Behavior."

my needs. Though Scripture tells us, "Do not love the world nor the things in the world," I find the lure of the world powerful (1 John 2:15). I know that "the lust of the flesh and the lust of the eyes and the boastful pride of life, is not from the Father, but is from the world" (1 John 2:16), yet I find myself drawn to it all nonetheless.

Materialism, sexual permissiveness, and pride not only run rampant in our society but also vie for position in my heart. Jesus calls us away from these pitfalls. Jesus' prayer for His disciples through all ages is: "I do not ask You to take them out of the world, but to keep them from the evil one. They are not of the world, even as I am not of the world" (John 17:15, 16). I need God's word to direct me like a light shining on the path, and I need the Holy Spirit to verify how God's commandment applies to my circumstances.

I have fooled myself into thinking that making spiritual decisions about my behavior would happen as naturally as boys grow attracted to girls, or someone gets hungry after several hours without food. Instead, I find it is more like wanting to eat healthfully—I cannot fully rely on my natural desires: they need to be educated, refined, and governed. I need to actively engage my will if I want to live above mere animal instinct. Practically speaking, I need to know how to live to stay connected to Christ and to demonstrate His character to the world.

Jesus said that all the law and prophets hang on the two concepts of loving the Lord our God with all our heart, soul, and mind, and loving our neighbor as ourselves. The application of those principles is not always as self-evident to me as it should be. So I take the first step in deciding how to live for Jesus in our society: I search the Bible. I look there to find direct counsel or a case study as an example on how to live a godly life in the circumstances I find myself in.

Since the Gospels describe God in the flesh, encountering everyday life experiences, I pay focused attention to the accounts of Jesus' life. I ask myself, "What would Jesus do?" Yet the world has changed so much from Jesus' day. He does not give us specifics on how to apply His love to our current times. The Bible doesn't tell us if Jesus would drive a bright-red sports car, get the latest model of cell phone, or play video games. So we need to consider how to apply principles to make decisions in these uncharted areas.

Principles and applications

Principles do not change, while applications may change with time, place, and culture. Let's imagine we have a principle of a house. I define "house" as a protective shelter with openings for leaving and entering. Location, materials available, economic considerations, and lifestyle needs can alter the application of "house." In Montana, a sprawling, ranch-style house makes sense. In a crammed city like Seattle, an apartment stacked on top of other homes better utilizes available space. Each fits the principle of "house," though the application differs greatly.

Applications may vary based on time, place, culture, and circumstances. God demands reverence from His people, and the principle to revere God stands for time and eternity. When He speaks to Moses before the burning bush, He makes the application, "Remove your sandals from your feet, for the place on which you are standing is holy ground" (Exodus 3:5). In Moses' culture, people took off their dusty, manure-covered shoes and had their feet washed before entering their host's home. This showed respect in not contaminating their host's home. Today, in polite society, taking off your shoes in church might be considered irreverent and disrespectful to God. In this case, the same principle might require the exact opposite application because of time and culture.

In the past, I have incorrectly given some applications the status of principles. For instance, I grew up in Yakima, Washington, where the prostitutes in the downtown area walked the streets during the fall and into the winter, wearing heavy makeup, miniskirts, high heels, and short, patchwork, rabbit-skin jackets. When I went to grad school at Andrews University and my girlfriend donned a patchwork, rabbit-skin jacket at the first cold snap, I dropped my jaw in repulsion, shocked at her indiscretion. She was confused at my insistence that she not wear it. She saw nothing wrong with the jacket, having grown up in a different area of the country without any negative association. Looking back, I see that the patchwork, rabbit-skin jacket was not *intrinsically* immoral. Because of its association for me, I took it as a statement of immorality.

We err when we take something that is immoral in application at a certain time and in a specific culture and proclaim it intrinsically immoral, thereby placing the application at the level of a principle. When we make our applications an absolute—treating them as principles—we run the risk of forgetting the principle. When burlesque theater—with its sexual innuendo and scantily clad women—became a popular entertainment, the Christian church spoke out, condemning theater. They didn't teach this as an application of the principles of *modesty*, *conformity* to the world, avoiding *lust*, or resisting addictive *enslavement*. The people who spoke for the church simply used their ecclesiastical authority to prohibit attendance by anyone wanting to stay in the fellowship as a Christian.

When theaters begin showing movies in the 1890s, the stigma stuck. In the Christian world, many took the application of not going to the movie house and made it the principle, viewing theaters as intrinsically wrong. So for years, genuine Christians, paying attention only to the application, skipped attending movies; however, when television came in the 1920s, they watched it unfiltered. They missed the underlying principle that by beholding we become changed (2 Corinthians 3:18). Now television goes much further in immorality, and people can watch pornography through their cable channels or Internet service. When the principle is taught of guarding what goes into the mind rather than the application of avoiding theaters, then Christians are able to wisely choose what to view, no matter what medium is used.

By teaching our children the principles behind our application, we are better able to give them tools to work through issues for themselves. The Bible does not specifically address the right or wrong of playing violent video games, how much time we should spend watching television, the use of anabolic steroids, if we should be involved in social media, or how much we should pay for a house. But God does give us case studies and specific principles for us to apply to our situation. Our youth need to know what principles to apply to issues ranging from bringing holograms into the home to making ethical choices in medical cloning.

This sampling of biblical principles helps me evaluate how to behave appropriately as a Christian.

» *Principle 1: Search.* After I pray for my heart to be open to God's leading, I search God's word for any direct counsel from God on the decision I have to make (2 Timothy 3:15, 16).

» *Principle 2: Weight.* I need to honestly decide if an action personally holds me back spiritually. "Let us also lay aside every weight" (Hebrews 12:1, 2, RSV).

» *Principle 3: Discerned.* Because spiritual things are spiritually discerned, I pray and ask for the leading of the Holy Spirit (1 Corinthians 2:14).

» *Principle 4: Example.* I need to consider how my actions will lead others in their Christian walk and avoid injuring a weaker brother (1 Corinthians 11:1; Romans 14:13).

» *Principle 5: Selfless.* I must check if an action puts others first. "Be devoted to one another in brotherly love; give preference to one another in honor" (Romans 12:10).

» *Principle 6: Revenge.* "Never take your own revenge, beloved, but leave room for the wrath of God, for it is written, 'Vengeance is Mine, I will repay,' says the Lord" (Romans 12:19).

» *Principle 7: Forgiveness.* I need to forgive and release old debts that I perceive others owe me. I no longer hold an account against someone who has wronged me (Matthew 18:21, 22).

» *Principle 8: Conformity.* "And do not be conformed to this world, but be transformed by the renewing of your mind, so that you may prove what the will of God is" (Romans 12:2).

» *Principle 9: Enslavement.* I must not choose something that will addict or enslave me or give Satan a stronghold in my life. We are slaves to the one we obey (Romans 6:16).

» *Principle 10: Purposeful.* I need to put all actions in line with the purpose God has given me for my life. "Not all things are profitable" for me (1 Corinthians 6:12).

» *Principle 11: Priority.* I must make God and His kingdom my first priority, putting everything else into place based on what serves His purposes best (Matthew 6:33).

» *Principle 12: Stewardship.* God owns me. He has assigned me the responsibility of managing the loaned money, time, talent, energy, and influence for Him (1 Corinthians 4:7).

» *Principle 13: Lust.* "Now flee from youthful lusts and pursue righteousness, faith, love and peace, with those who call on the Lord from a pure heart" (2 Timothy 2:22).

» *Principle 14: Authority.* I must recognize that earthly authority comes from God (Romans 13:1). Unless it conflicts with my Christian convictions, I must obey civil authorities (Mark 12:17).

» *Principle 15: Temple.* God lives in my body, His temple. My body belongs to Him. I choose each action to benefit my emotional, physical, and spiritual well-being (1 Corinthians 6:19).

» *Principle 16: Incompatibility.* I will not bind myself to an unbeliever in a way that gives him or her the ability to prohibit me from following my conscience before God (2 Corinthians 6:14).

» *Principle 17: Evangelism.* I will conduct myself in a way to use the opportunity to bring unbelievers to a saving relationship with Jesus (Colossians 4:5).

» *Principle 18: Imitate.* I should determine how Jesus would respond in a situation and "walk in the same manner as He walked" (1 John 2:6).

» *Principle 19: Beholding.* I must censor what I put into my mind through my senses; this shapes my thoughts, and thoughts shape my actions (2 Corinthians 3:18; Philippians 4:8).

» *Principle 20: Appearance.* "Therefore do not let what is for you a good thing be spoken of as evil" (Romans 14:16). "Abstain from all appearance of evil" (1 Thessalonians 5:22 KJV).

» *Principle 21: Judging.* Do not judge others' hearts, but discern if the actions they perform comply with God's commands and principles. We judge sin but not the sinner (Matthew 7:1–3; John 7:24).

» *Principle 22: Modesty.* I should not distract people from seeing the God who lives inside of me by outside show (1 Timothy 2:9, 10; 1 Peter 3:3, 4).

We will continue to grow in our application of Christian principles in our lives. The Bible doesn't offer multiple lifestyles. It argues that either we have selected a lifestyle with Jesus or we have selected a "deathstyle" apart from Him. We no longer live just to please ourselves. No longer do we ask what will bring us happiness, pleasure, or immediate satisfaction as the ultimate question. The real question: will we glorify the Lord in how we live? "Whether, then, you eat or drink or whatever you do, do all to the glory of God" (1 Corinthians 10:31). I find a God beyond my wildest dreams who wants to live through me.

Thoughts to Ponder

1. In what circumstances have I seen others take an application and make it a principle? In what areas have I taken a standard or application and dealt with it as a principle?

_____

_____

_____

2. How often do I judge others' spirituality by their outside behavior? Has there been a time when my assumptions about their spiritual walk were later proven to be wrong?

_____

_____

_____

3. Am I more likely to fall into "legalistic judgment" or "liberal rationalism"? Where do I see this happening right now in my life?

_____

_____

_____

4. Looking at the list of principles, how would I prioritize them?

_____

_____

_____

5. Is there a benefit to sitting down and discussing how someone else applies biblical principles as a Christian? With whom might I sit down and hear how they observe the Sabbath or apply the principles of health to their life?

_____

_____

_____

CHAPTER 10

God Makes Me Whole

A group of ancient Gnostic holy men strove to free their divine spirits by subjugating their "evil" physical bodies—forsaking physical pleasure, living in caves, wearing only sackcloth, sleeping on beds of nails, whipping themselves, and eating only enough to sustain them.

Others took the same philosophical concept of a separated body and mind to an opposite extreme. They indulged in physical pleasure, held feasts, lived licentiously, and participated in drunken orgies, eagerly anticipating that in the end their bodies would die and their spirits would soar. They believed they could immerse the flesh in base living and allow their spirits to live in a higher, disconnected plane of reality.

God created us as whole beings

God's perspective comes as a sharp contrast to both of these philosophies. He explains that He designed us as whole beings: spirit, soul, and body—interconnected and interdependent—in one being (1 Thessalonians 5:23). Humans *became* living beings; they do not *have* a living being (Genesis 2:7). From the day of our creation, we have a physical body as part of our form. Our thoughts and emotions depend on a physical brain, and we do not exist apart from this physical being.

And while God promises to transform or resurrect our body, we look forward to a physical existence (1 Corinthians 15:42–44). We will have physical bodies just as Jesus had a real physical resurrected body, which the disciples touched (Luke 24:41–43; John 20:27).

We do not own or possess our own bodies (1 Corinthians 6:19). Paul counseled his readers, you "have been bought with a price: therefore glorify God in your body" (1 Corinthians 6:20). People argue, "It's my body; I have the right to do with it what I want." But the Bible says every aspect of you belongs to God.

Some still believe in a compartmentalized physical and spiritual life. People retort, "Whether I eat right, exercise, drink occasionally, take drugs recreationally, or get fat has nothing to do with my spirituality." God strongly counters: "Whether, then, you eat or drink or whatever you do, do all to the glory of God" (1 Corinthians 10:31).

God fashioned us to house His presence. From the beginning, He intended not to just live beside us but in us. "Do you not know that you are a temple of God and that the Spirit of God dwells in you? . . . For the temple of God is holy, and that is what you are" (1 Corinthians 3:16, 17). God sanctified us for His use. He intends to use us as an opportunity to connect sinful humanity with divinity. Through contact with us, others meet the "resident" God.

This chapter is based on Seventh-day Adventist fundamental belief no. 22, "Christian Behavior."

God wants us healthy while we live as His temple, but He also desires to give us the benefits of health because He loves us and want to spare us from pain.

God seeks to restore us to wholeness

The word in the Greek translated "to save" from sin is *sozo*. "For the Son of Man has come *to save* that which was lost" (Matthew 18:11; emphasis added). Exactly the same word Scripture translates as "to heal" in the following text in the NIV. "He said to her, 'Daughter, your faith has *healed* you' " (Mark 5:34; emphasis added). Both physical healing and spiritual saving come from a word that means "to restore to wholeness."

Anything that affects our physical body affects our emotions and mind and therefore affects our relationship with God. Thinking of a lemon causes a physical response in my mouth. Fear can cause a ninety-pound woman to release adrenaline that enables her to lift a car. Sickness or pain can make me prone to irritability. There is a direct connection between the physical, mental, emotional, and spiritual elements of our person. So taking care of our physical body affects us spiritually.

Our heavenly Designer gave specific instruction on how to care for His temple, including what we should and shouldn't eat and drink. If I want my new car to function optimally, I must pay attention to the manufacturer's manual. It details the kind of oil and gas the engine takes and the schedule of service maintenance required. We don't have to follow the manual, but then the manufacturer no longer bears the responsibility for the malfunctioning of the machine. We can decide to put water in the gas tank, but the car won't run.

Specific health principles

We will use NEWSTART[1] as an acronym to focus on health principles that will help us to live longer. These health principles come from both science and the Bible.

Nutrition: Nutrition focuses on what we should feed our bodies. In 1992, the USDA published the food pyramid, which replaced the chart of four basic food groups in an attempt to educate the public on the portions and the selection of foods we should eat. "The first chart suggested to the USDA by nutritional experts in 1992 featured fruits and vegetables as the biggest group, not breads. This chart was overturned at the hand of special interests in the grain, meat, and dairy industries, all of which are heavily subsidized by the USDA."[2] Even though interests somewhat altered, the chart's most basic health principles prevailed: increase vegetable and fruit intake and reduce fat, cholesterol, sugar, and salt consumption. Choose complex carbohydrates with the whole grain rather than refined carbohydrates. For me, this translates into choosing wheat bread over white and selecting full-grain pastas and tortillas that are made from whole-grain flour.

God's original diet consisted of vegetables, seeds, and fruit. "Then God said, 'Behold, I have given you every plant yielding seed that is on the surface of all the earth, and every tree which has fruit yielding seed; it shall be food for you' " (Genesis 1:29). "And you will eat the plants of the field" (Genesis 3:18).

After the Flood, meat was introduced: "Every moving thing that is alive shall be food for you; I give all to you, as I gave the green plant" (Genesis 9:3). Some have questioned if this literally meant anything that moved could be killed and eaten as long as the blood is drained (Genesis 9:4). If so, God was giving permission for Noah to eat other men, women, and children. This goes against God's law, common sense, and integrity. God authorized eating creatures in the same way He extended the eating of green plants. Not all green plants will give us health. Some can kill us. Just as some plants were never intended to be eaten, some animals were never intended to be food.

God later clarified which animals would work as food and which would not. While He mentions specific animals throughout the chapter, three main principles help us to sort out animals that were not intended for food (Leviticus 11; Deuteronomy 14).

Acceptable land animals to use for food. "Whatever divides a hoof, thus making split hoofs, and chews the cud, among the animals, that you may eat" (Leviticus 11:3). This principle does exclude some things people eat, including rabbit, possum, and pork.

Acceptable water creatures to use for food. "Whatever in the water does not have fins and scales is abhorrent to you" (Leviticus 11:12). Stated positively, if it has fins and scales, it's edible. This excludes eating catfish, crab, lobster, shrimp, octopus, squid, oysters, eel, and clams. Most of us recognize these creatures as "bottom feeders," which primarily function as the filtration system of the sea. God also designates the shark, swordfish, and whale as unclean.

Acceptable air creatures to use for food. The eagle, the vulture, the buzzard, and the hawk stand among the birds specifically mentioned as unfit for eating (Leviticus 11:13–16). Birds like the chicken, the quail, the turkey, and the pheasant may be eaten.

The clean and unclean distinction did not pertain merely to the ceremonial law for sacrifice. When God instructed Noah to take the animals into the ark, He said, "You shall take with you of every clean animal by sevens, a male and his female; and of the animals that are not clean two, a male and his female" (Genesis 7:2).

The distinction between clean and unclean animals was present before a ceremonial law was given and before the Jewish nation existed! If Noah and his family had eaten unclean animals immediately after the Flood, we would have no unclean animals since they were taken into the ark in pairs. The clean were taken in by seven pairs. They therefore could sacrifice them, eat them, and still have a breeding pair to maintain the species.

Exercise: One of the greatest factors affecting health is exercise. The Centers for Disease Control and Prevention sets a goal for adults: moderate to intense aerobic exercise for "2 hours and 30 minutes" per week.[3] You can fill this weekly target by reaching and sustaining your target heart rate for thirty minutes at least five times a week. Exercise increases the production of endorphins, which are natural mood elevators. It aids in increasing metabolism and thereby weight management. It helps to prevent cardiovascular diseases, sleeping disorders, depression, type 2 diabetes, stroke, arthritis, and select cancers.

Water: Water makes up 50 to 60 percent of our body weight. It has an essential role in almost every system of the body. Cells and tissue depend on water to transport and supply nutrients. Chemical and metabolic reactions need water to function. The body regulates its temperature through water exchange and secretion. Water serves as a means to eliminate toxins and waste built up inside. If you're not sure about your hydration level, look at your urine. If your urine is clear, you probably drink sufficient water.

Many health experts today recommend drinking at least six to eight eight-ounce glasses of water per day or approximately a half gallon. Water not only cleanses but also provides increased circulation and relaxation.

Sunshine: Sun exposure has received bad press because overexposure to the sun damages skin and promotes skin cancer. However, the sun actually heals and prevents many skin diseases with proper monitoring of exposure. A "study links UVB as protective to a total of 16 types of cancer."[4] People living in areas with longer hours of daylight have fewer occurrences of colon cancer, Hodgkin's lymphoma, ovarian cancer, pancreatic, and prostate cancer. When we have controlled exposure to the sun's ultraviolet rays, it kills germs, stimulates the production of vitamin D, reduces the heart rate, increases the heart's stroke volume, slows respiration, and lowers blood pressure. In addition, exposure to sunlight elevates the mood and produces calm. It prompts the brain to increase the production of both serotonin and melatonin, which aid in the sleep cycle and the setting of the circadian rhythm.[5]

Temperance: Temperance means to abstain from that which would destroy and to balance or moderate exposure so the most positive results will be obtained. We can have too much of even a good thing. For example, the Bible condemns overeating (Proverbs 23:1, 2). In other things, the Bible calls for complete abstinence.

Regarding alcohol, the Bible says, "Wine is a mocker, strong drink a brawler, and whoever is intoxicated by it is not wise" (Proverbs 20:1). In Old Testament times, drinking had the same intoxicating effects it does now (Proverbs 23:29–35). Scripture says that no "drunkards . . . will inherit the kingdom of God" (1 Corinthians 6:10). The Greek word translated as drunkard, *methysos*, means "one that becomes intoxicated." We often redefine it to mean "fall down drunk," but it refers to one who uses alcohol for intoxication. How much do I need to have drunk to be considered intoxicated? Federal aviation regulations do not allow a pilot to fly a plane within eight hours of drinking *any* alcohol. According to federal aviation regulation 91.17, a pilot is considered impaired with a blood alcohol level at 0.04 percent or greater.[6] This measure of intoxication is half the usual legal limit for operating a motor vehicle. The average person might appear completely functional at this level but would still be considered intoxicated by the aviation board. To be intoxicated means to have a compromised judgment or the diminished capacity to act from being under the influence of alcohol.

The *New York Daily News* reports, "Roughly three in 10 U.S. adults have a drinking problem or have misused alcohol at some point in the past."[7] Regular sustained drinking is linked to loss of memory, judgment, and learning ability.

How does alcohol produce opposite reactions, with some "happy drunks" and some "angry drunks"? The first drink acts on the frontal lobe of the brain, which serves as our action inhibitor and gives us the ability to govern our actions, our speech, and our thoughts. Here we choose to override our animal passions. We don't have to beat someone up when angry or flirt when someone attracts us. In our frontal lobe, we can override our natural inclination with a moral code of operation.

With the frontal lobe chemically impaired, the intoxicated person becomes less inhibited and more likely to fall into temptation. As Christians, we seek to make moral decisions based on our understanding of the principles of love. We need all of our brain power. God calls us to lay aside every weight or "encumbrance" to being fully yielded to Jesus (Hebrews 12:1, 2).

Smoking is another form of substance abuse. In short, cigarettes provide suicide on an installment plan. Cigarettes contain nicotine, carbon monoxide, cadmium, ammonia, benzene, hydrogen cyanide, and other poisonous chemicals. One of the Ten Commandments tells us, "You shall not murder" (Exodus 20:13). Smoking steals life not only from the smoker but also the life of a loved one. Both of my parents died of cancer—a direct result of their choice to smoke heavily. Cigarettes do not just take years off your life, but they also steal the quality of your life. For the last ten years of my mother's life, she moved around while tethered to an oxygen tank. Chewing tobacco changes some of the affected parts of the body, and cancers of the lip, throat, stomach, and bowel are greatly increased. Moreover, cigarettes and tobacco become the master that rules over the slave in addiction.

Although accepted culturally, caffeine also constitutes drug usage. Caffeine remains one of the most widely consumed central nervous system stimulants and psychoactive drugs in the world. It is legal, virtually unregulated, and socially acceptable. It has been found to contribute to high blood cholesterol, high blood pressure, peptic ulcers, sleeplessness, headaches, and increased anxiety and panic disorders. And it has been implicated in heart disease, diabetes, and cancer of the colon, bladder, and pancreas.

Christians should abstain from any chemical used recreationally rather than medicinally. The negative effects of marijuana have been increasingly downplayed. Studies reveal marijuana use has been linked to damage of the lungs, memory, and mental health. The facts repudiate the claims by some that smoking marijuana presents fewer health risks than smoking cigarettes. "Smoking one joint is equal to smoking five cigarettes—smoking four joints is like smoking an entire pack."[8] This increases the risk for infection of the lungs and chronic cough.

The very thing that gives marijuana smokers their high also changes their brain chemistry. The THC (tetrahydrocannabinol) from smoking damages neurotransmitters and in the long term creates the effects of a "pot head." Users exhibit lack of motivation, slow processing, diminished focus, and low memory retention.

While some feel caught in the cycle of addiction, God promises, "For freedom Christ has set us free; stand firm therefore, and do not submit again to a yoke of slavery" (Galatians 5:1, ESV).

Air: Breathing fresh air deeply provides multiple benefits to your body. Deep breathing includes inhaling through your nose, expanding your stomach and filling your chest, holding for the count of three, and then exhaling through the slightly open lips. It releases tension and releases carbon dioxide. Relaxing the mind helps to relieve emotional stress. Oxygen feeds the muscles—especially the brain—and strengthens the immune system. It increases organ function, assists in weight loss, and improves both the digestion and nervous system.

Rest: Real rest produces a pleasant, comfortable state of well-being. Rest gives the cells and muscles a chance to repair. The body does most of its repair when demands have decreased. Eight hours of sleep is the average need for a body. The biblical balance of work and worship is essential (Exodus 20:9, 10).

Trust in God: As we enter this journey of life, God calls us to trust in Him and allow Him to move for us. Emotional strength, peace, and stability can be a major factor in total health. There is joy in Christ (Proverbs 17:22; 4:20–22).

We present our lives as living sacrifices to God to demonstrate our trust. "Therefore I urge you, brethren, by the mercies of God, to present your bodies a living and holy sacrifice, acceptable to God, which is your spiritual service of worship. And do not be conformed to this world, but be transformed by the renewing of your mind, so that you may prove what the will of God is, that which is good and acceptable and perfect" (Romans 12:1–3).

We should live in a way that demonstrates our appreciation for Christ's sacrifice on our behalf. God brings change to our life through communicating truths in our mind. We should sacrifice to God anything that damages God's ability to communicate to our mind.

God seeks to bless us, desiring to restore us to wholeness. When we follow His plan, we reap the benefits. "Seventh-day Adventists . . . live an average of 10 years longer than the American life expectancy of about 79 years."[9] God wants to give us not only longer life but also a better life. He says, "I came that they may have life, and have it abundantly" (John 10:10). That's the God beyond my wildest dreams.

1. "What Is NEWSTART?" Weimar Institute, accessed November 2, 2016, http://newstart.com/what-is-newstart1/#sthash.m5gsvyPb .dpbs.

2. "History of Nutritional Guidelines: Controversy," *Wikipedia*, last modified April 16, 2016, https://en.wikipedia.org/wiki/History_of _USDA_nutrition_guides.

3. Centers for Disease Control and Prevention, "How Much Physical Activity Do Adults Need?" CDC, last modified June 4, 2015, http://www.cdc.gov/physicalactivity/basics/adults/index.htm.

4. William B. Grant, "Reduce Your Risk of Cancer With Sunlight Exposure," Mercola.com, March 31, 2004, http://articles.mercola .com/sites/articles/archive/2004/03/31/cancer-sunlight.aspx.

5. Ibid.

6. Federal Aviation Administration, "Code of Federal Regulations: Part 91 General Operating and Flight Rules," accessed June 30, 2016, http://fgl.faa.gov/Regulatory_and_Guidance_Library/rgFAR.nsf/0/28757d8ae4d7d671862571960066be86!OpenDocument.

7. Reuters, "Three in 10 American Adults Have a Drinking Problem: Study," *New York Daily News*, June 8, 2015, http://www .nydailynews.com/life-style/health/10-american-adults-drinking-problem-study-article-1.2250854.

8. American Univeristy Wellness Center, "Marijuana," American University, accessed May 21, 2016, http://www.american.edu/ocl/ wellness/Marijuana.cfm.

9. Ryan Buxton, "What Seventh-day Adventists Get Right That Lengthens Their Life Expectancy," *Huffington Post*, July 31, 2014, http:// www.huffingtonpost.com/2014/07/31/seventh-day-adventists-life-expectancy_n_5638098.html.

Thoughts to Ponder

1. Have I thought of my physical body as part of my spiritual life? The words for "save" and "heal" are the same in the original biblical language. How does that understanding connect my spiritual and physical health?

_____

_____

_____

2. What element of NEWSTART do I need to focus on to be in better physical health?

_____

_____

_____

3. Does making an effort to overcome destructive habits seem legalistic? What are the specific goals I would like to set to advance health wise?

_____

_____

_____

4. Who might I recruit as an accountability partner for growing in my health practices?

_____

_____

_____

5. Have I been making excuses, or rationalizations, for not taking the steps I need health-wise? Am I ready now? How does trust in divine power affect my physical health?

_____

_____

_____

CHAPTER 11

Security as His Managers

Dad's sudden phone call whisked him away, preventing him from taking my brothers and me to get Mom's birthday present. Since the next day was Mom's birthday, she had to fill in for Dad. At the store, she announced she would be in the men's department, which allowed her four boys free run of the rest of the store with the five dollars she gave to each of us to spend.

The situation struck me as paradoxical: Mom gave us her own money to buy her a gift. I don't remember what I bought her, but I am sure she could have used the five dollars and bought herself something that would have better met her needs or fancy.

As Mom opened the gift, smile lines accented her eyes as the sentiments of the token touched her heart. In that instant, I found the joy of giving even with borrowed money. The opportunity to return what had been given me allowed me to express my love to her.

"The earth is the LORD's, and all it contains, the world, and those who dwell in it" (Psalm 24:1). Our heavenly Father owns everything. He possesses the "cattle on a thousand hills" (Psalm 50:10), the silver and gold (Haggai 2:8), and the people themselves who dwell on the earth (Psalm 100:3). We cannot increase God's holdings by giving back what belongs to Him. The benefit that comes to God and to us is found in the heartfelt expression of gratitude.

God assigned Adam and Eve the responsibility to rule over the animals and to manage and take care of the garden (Genesis 1:28; 2:15). The tree of the knowledge of good and evil allowed Adam and Eve to acknowledge God's ownership by observing His restriction. God had reserved the tree for Himself. In return, they experienced a sense of total security knowing that God would meet their needs.

After the fall of mankind, God chose a different way to give humans an opportunity to demonstrate their trust in Him. "Thus all the tithe of the land, of the seed of the land or of the fruit of the tree, is the LORD's; it is holy to the LORD" (Leviticus 27:30). Returning a tithe to God became the symbol of recognizing that He supplies all of our needs.

Just as He set one-seventh of time (the seventh-day Sabbath) aside as belonging to Him, so He has set one-tenth of our gain apart as belonging to Him. The percentage makes His command equitable for the poor and rich. The tithe belongs to God. To keep it for our own purposes constitutes stealing (Malachi 3:8, 9). God does not appeal to our sense of gratitude or generosity *to give* tithe but to our sense of loyalty and honesty *to return* tithe.

Our returning tithe makes a difference to God. Our obedient response brings God joy (1 Samuel 15:22). It constitutes a statement of commitment, loyalty, and understanding.

This chapter is based on Seventh-day Adventist fundamental belief no. 21, "Stewardship."

God responds by committing Himself to meet our needs. " 'Bring the whole tithe into the storehouse, so that there may be food in My house, and test Me now in this,' says the LORD of hosts, 'if I will not open for you the windows of heaven and pour out for you a blessing until it overflows' " (Malachi 3:10). These words confirm God's desire to shower His faithful with the blessings that fill His storehouses.

He promises the gift in overflowing abundance. If we honor God first, He will pour out heaven's richest blessings (Proverbs 3:9, 10). Additionally, "honor the LORD from your wealth and from the first of all your produce; so your barns will be filled with plenty and your vats will overflow with new wine" (Proverbs 3:9, 10).

With this abundant increase, all the nations will recognize a supernatural blessing that will enable us to share about our Lord (Malachi 3:12). From the beginning, God placed His people Israel as a hub in the midst of the Middle East so that as nations traveled through they would see the hand of the Lord with Israel. God trusts us to acknowledge Him as providing the good gifts and not to think that they have come from our power or through our efforts (Deuteronomy 8:11, 17).

Sometimes we view money as if it will fill our needs. People rely on money as their security, their source of pleasure, their power, and their god. Even Christians find that they naturally gravitate toward prioritizing money. Jesus told a parable of a man who made wealth his security. This man finds he has more than he needs and decides to build bigger barns. In his delight, he announces, "Soul, you have many goods laid up for many years to come; take your ease, eat, drink and be merry" (Luke 12:19). In the parable, the man loses his life that very night.

God did not condemn the man because he saved his wealth. After all, He instructed Joseph to store Egypt's wealth in the prosperous years in preparation for the years of famine. But this man relied on his wealth to be his security—not on God.

Being significantly frugal, I naturally save for future projects. I saved for my own college tuition, saved for a down payment on a house, and saved for the kids' college tuition. Now I save for retirement. Part of my plight as a saver is that I can't seem to save enough. Intellectually, I know that I cannot trust in my money—a stock market downturn could devalue my investments overnight. I am learning how to find my security in Jesus and not in money. God created us so we would enjoy pleasures, but He knows that only our connection with Him will bring us unending joy.

Simon the sorcerer attempted to use money to buy power and gain a sense of value. When he witnessed the power of the Holy Spirit that came at the apostles' laying on of hands, he wanted it. "He offered them money, saying, 'Give this authority to me as well, so that everyone on whom I lay my hands may receive the Holy Spirit' " (Acts 8:18, 19). How easily we confuse the purpose of money. While money may be used to advance God's kingdom, it does not have power in the spiritual world. "For there is no respect of persons with God" (Romans 2:11, KJV). We may use money to command respect, feel important, or to convince ourselves of our value, but ultimately God will override human plans and schemes.

Jacob used money to pay the bride price for the love of his life. He worked seven years and used the wages to pay Rachel's dowry (Genesis 29:16–28). Even today, money still serves as an enticement for marriage. Money can buy a companion, but it cannot buy genuine love.

These natural methods of using money assume that money can meet our needs, but in the end they dethrone God. Job realized this: "If I have put my trust in gold or said to pure gold, 'You are my security,' if I have rejoiced over my great wealth, the fortune my hands had gained . . . then these also would be sins to be judged, for I would have been unfaithful to God on high" (Job 31:24–28, NIV). Jesus reiterates this truth in the Sermon on the Mount: "No one can serve two masters. . . . You cannot serve God and wealth" (Matthew 6:24).

This truth challenges me to examine my life. Am I following God or money or trying to serve both? My use of money indicates whether I have died to self or not. I have entered into a partnership with God when I come to the place I am ready to manage the money not just for myself but for God's cause. Then I begin to think in terms of kingdom results. God commands me to "seek first His kingdom and His righteousness, and all these things will be added to you" (Matthew 6:33).

When my wife and I struggle financially, or have a loss of property, we remind ourselves that it's all going to burn (2 Peter 3:10). In the end, everything we have will burn. And before that, persecution toward Christians may require us to walk away from what we have in order to flee to some secluded place. In that day, only the money we used in our partnership with God to bring mankind toward Him will have a lasting impact.

Our tithe demonstrates our allegiance to and trust in God, and it goes to advance His kingdom. From its initial introduction, tithing went to the priests to sustain them as they ministered to His people (Numbers 18:21–24). In an economy where possessions and property were exchanged more than money, God set up a system to support those who were set aside for ministry. The priests of the tribe of Levi were to spend their full time in ministry. The other eleven tribes gave 10 percent of their income, or increase, to support those ordained to ministry. Paul argued that the Lord Himself had established as a principle that "those who proclaim the gospel . . . get their living from the gospel" (1 Corinthians 9:14). Writers, poets, counselors, and singers get their income from the work they produce. Those whom God ordained to full-time gospel ministry should also receive benefit for their work. Since tithe goes to pay those whom He set aside to spread the message, tithe paying directly supports the work of God. God has ordained the church as the storehouse to orchestrate the distribution of the tithe funds for ministry (Malachi 3:10).

The storehouse is God's organized church. As Christians, we return tithe to the organized church that holds the greatest biblical truth. That body then distributes the funds to its duly called ministers. We return God's tithe to His church. If an individual withholds tithe, that person robs God (Malachi 3:8).

Carrying out God's work requires more than the tithe. God has partnered with us to give offerings as well. To give no offerings constitutes robbing God just as much as withholding tithe (Malachi 3:8). Offerings we give to God in gratitude and for the advancement of His kingdom. How much should we give? Scripture doesn't give a specific amount. I like the counsel given to the Israelites when they would come together for the annual feasts: "Every man shall give as he is able, according to the blessing of the LORD your God which He has given you" (Deuteronomy 16:17).

Offerings cover everything that the tithe doesn't. Church-budget offerings pay for the general operating of the church. These funds cover everything from heat, air conditioning, lights, maintenance, quarterlies, bulletins, and secretary salary to janitors, groundskeeping, and photocopying. In addition, special offerings allow ministries for evangelism, camp, youth programs, building projects, new equipment, the poor, and education costs. Sometimes I get overwhelmed thinking of the financial needs to carry out God's work. But I am reminded that "one gives freely, yet grows all the richer; another withholds what he should give, and only suffers want. Whoever brings blessing will be enriched, and one who waters will himself be watered" (Proverbs 11:24, 25, ESV).

As I partner with God, my heart tunes to His. In choosing to give tithes and offerings, I discipline myself to deny myself for His cause. God does not say, "Put your money where your heart is." Instead He says, "For where your treasure is, there your heart will be also" (Matthew 6:21, ESV). In other words, we choose where to put our treasure (money), and our heart will follow. In love for Him, I choose to become generous. "Now this I say, he who sows sparingly will also reap sparingly, and he who sows bountifully will also reap bountifully. Each one must do just as he has purposed in his heart, not grudgingly or under compulsion, for God loves a cheerful giver" (2 Corinthians 9:6, 7). I am able to give cheerfully because I delight in advancing Jesus' kingdom.

God provides this counsel for the wealthy: "Instruct those who are rich in this present world not to be conceited or to fix their hope on the uncertainty of riches, but on God, who richly supplies us with all things to enjoy. Instruct them to do good, to be rich in good works, to be generous and ready to share, storing up for themselves the treasure of a good foundation for the future, so that they may take hold of that which is life indeed" (1 Timothy 6:17–19).

God is our security. He owns us and provides for our needs. He has entrusted to us the earth and our strength, ability, and possessions to manage for the benefit of His kingdom. He has commanded we return 10 percent of our income as recognition of His ownership and offerings based on our increase. When we give ourselves totally to Him, we partner with Him and find the same joy in giving toward the restoration of God and His people. The God beyond my wildest dreams lives as my Benefactor.

Thoughts to Ponder

1. Do I naturally use money to buy power, security, pleasure, or love?

_____

_____

_____

2. If someone were to track my money, where would they find my priorities? How much do I use money to support building the cause of God?

_____

_____

_____

3. Where have I seen God meeting my financial needs in the past? Have I tested Him by being faithful in returning both tithe and offerings?

_____

_____

_____

4. Do I give systematically or in response to need? Do I give by percentage? Do I rely on others to fund the church budget and Adventist education, while I give only to projects? If people gave as I give, would God's ministries be sustained?

_____

_____

_____

5. When I tithe, I am saying I acknowledge that all the money God has entrusted to me belongs to Him. Do I give out of my surplus or sacrificially? Do I live as if I were managing God's money for Him, or as if I were managing my own money?

_____

_____

_____

CHAPTER 12

The Profit of a Prophet

C risis struck the nation—the Syrians, Ammonites, and Moabites had banded together to destroy Judah. To his credit, King Jehoshaphat recognized that he did not possess the power to win this battle. He called the nation together to seek God's direction. The king pleaded with God before the people, saying, "We are powerless before this great multitude who are coming against us; nor do we know what to do, but our eyes are on You" (2 Chronicles 20:12).

Then the Spirit of the Lord was poured upon the prophet Jahaziel, who served as God's mouthpiece, and he said, "Do not fear . . . for the battle is not yours, but God's" (2 Chronicles 20:15). Through Jahaziel, whose name means "beheld by God," God issued specific instructions. The people would not fight. God would fight for them. Jehoshaphat bowed and worshiped God, and the people joined him (2 Chronicles 20:18).

The next morning the king proclaimed, "Put your trust in the LORD your God and you will be established. Put your trust in His prophets and succeed" (2 Chronicles 20:20). The king believed so completely in God's prophet and his message that he replaced his frontline soldiers with a choir (2 Chronicles 20:21). And the Lord acted for them and destroyed their enemy.

They placed their lives on the line based on the words of a prophet. This prophet foretold the future and gave specific directions.

A prophet's function
God the Holy Spirit moved upon the authors of Scripture to communicate His word to His people. The same Holy Spirit authored both the Old and New Testaments. The Spirit moved men to chronicle God's acts in history so they might serve as an example to us. The purpose of the Word is to bring us to a saving knowledge and relationship with God—the Father, Son, and Holy Spirit. "All Scripture is inspired by God and profitable for teaching, for reproof, for correction, for training in righteousness; so that the man of God may be adequate, equipped for every good work" (2 Timothy 3:16, 17). As the final authority in our lives, it proves the infallible revelation of God's will, recorded in case studies and specific doctrines. But we still need the Holy Spirit to function; the gift of prophecy has not stopped with the giving of Scripture.

God used prophets in a variety of capacities. But all God's prophets then and now have a common purpose—they communicate God's will to the people. "He said, 'Hear now My words: If there is a prophet among you, I, the LORD, shall make Myself known to him in

This chapter is based on Seventh-day Adventist fundamental beliefs no. 1, "The Holy Scriptures"; and no. 18, "The Gift of Prophecy."

a vision. I shall speak with him in a dream' " (Numbers 12:6). "Surely the Lord GOD does nothing unless He reveals His secret counsel to His servants the prophets" (Amos 3:7).

God uses different means to give His message. Sometimes He gives visions; other times He works in dreams; He even plants thoughts in people's minds. He uses prophets to instruct in living parables and at times speaks to them face-to-face (Hosea 12:10; Daniel 7:2). A prophet speaks for God on His behalf. Speaking on God's behalf at times requires God to share His foreknowledge in order to move the people in the direction He desires. In other instances, He uses the prophet to call them to return to His previously revealed will. The prophet may just serve as His mouthpiece to confirm or encourage His people that they need to continue to follow His will in the midst of hardship.

Jesus warns against false prophets. "For false Christs and false prophets will arise and will show great signs and wonders, so as to mislead, if possible, even the elect" (Matthew 24:24).

The warning against false prophets indicates there must be true prophets. Otherwise, Jesus could have just told us to not listen to prophets at all. God calls prophets to lose sight of themselves. Often He instructs them to deliver messages of rebuke, which make them unpopular with the people. False prophets, such as Balaam and Hananiah, seek popularity. God says of them: "Thus says the LORD of hosts, 'Do not listen to the words of the prophets who are prophesying to you. They are leading you into futility; they speak a vision of their own imagination, not from the mouth of the LORD' "(Jeremiah 23:16).

While we need to guard against false prophets today, we seem to fall into a greater danger of ignoring the true prophets He has given us. God told us, "Do not quench the Spirit; do not despise prophetic utterances" (1 Thessalonians 5:19, 20). Throughout its history, Israel ignored the message of God through His prophets, leading Jesus to cry, "Jerusalem, Jerusalem, who kills the prophets and stones those who are sent to her! How often I wanted to gather your children together, the way a hen gathers her chicks under her wings, and you were unwilling" (Matthew 23:37). God, in compassion, has sent messengers to correct and direct His people. When they refused the messengers, they refused the message of God.

God can use prophets today to continue to direct us in the right way. Even with the Bible, there is the contemporary need to hear God's instruction.

The prophet serves as God's voice leading the people

God employs prophets to lead His church and to help guard His people against false doctrine and worldly corruption. "One who prophesies edifies the church" (1 Corinthians 14:4). Through the Holy Spirit He poured out the gift of prophecy to aid in the same work as evangelists, pastors, and teachers, "for the equipping of the saints for the work of service, to the building up of the body of Christ" (Ephesians 4:12).

This gift will function "until we all attain to the unity of the faith, and of the knowledge of the Son of God, to a mature man, to the measure of the stature which belongs to the fullness of Christ" (Ephesians 4:13). "As a result, we are no longer to be children, tossed here and there by waves and carried about by every wind of doctrine, by the trickery of man, by craftiness in deceitful scheming" (Ephesians 4:14). As yet we do not find ourselves united in faith or knowledge about Jesus or grown to maturity; therefore, the gift must still be necessary. God lists prophecy as one of the gifts He gives through the Spirit (1 Corinthians 12:10, 11, 28).

As a five-year-old child, I remember thinking I would run free, so I closed my eyes and ran from the back door through our backyard, arms straight out at my sides like an airplane, and I ran headfirst into the only tree in our backyard. To ignore prophecy would be like running with our eyes closed—just as I did. God's prophets guard His people.

God calls His prophets at times to minister to a specific group of people at a certain time and through a specific circumstance. He preserves their writings and stories to work with people through all time. Moses led the entire nation of Israel on God's behalf. We attribute the main body of the Pentateuch (the first five books of the Bible) to him. Moses' siblings Aaron and Miriam also worked beside him with the prophetic gift, but they did not write anything that was preserved for us to read (Exodus 7:1).

Other prophets wrote counsel on God's behalf. These were inspired writings given to specific people. But God did not see fit to preserve them for us. "Now the acts of King David, from first to last, are written in the chronicles of Samuel the seer, in the chronicles of Nathan the prophet and in the chronicles of Gad the seer" (1 Chronicles 29:29). Nathan the prophet worked as a true prophet, but we do not have a biblical book of Nathan. The Bible notes other inspired writings, including the book of Enoch (Jude 14), Paul's letter to Laodicea (Colossians 4:16), the book of Jasher (Joshua 10:13), and the book of Shemaiah the prophet and Iddo the seer (2 Chronicles 12:15; 13:22). Evidently God did not consider these essential for us today. God may limit a prophet's work or influence to a specific time and people.

Prophetess

At times, God chose to work through a female prophetess. "Now Deborah, a prophetess, the wife of Lappidoth, was judging Israel at that time" (Judges 4:4). In choosing Deborah, God broadened our understanding of the prophetic role. In the midst of the male-dominated culture of biblical times, God gave the gift of prophecy to a woman, just as He had earlier with Miriam. Scripture also records Huldah (2 Kings 22), Anna (Luke 2:36), and the daughters of Phillip (Acts 21:8, 9) all receiving this prophetic gift from God.

In Deborah's case, it included the role of judge. God placed her as the supreme spiritual and civil leader of Israel in her time. Truly, prophets can serve as military and civil leaders as well as speak and lead on God's behalf. The gift can be given to men, women, children, and even, in one circumstance, a donkey (Joel 2:28; Acts 2:17; Numbers 22:28).

The confirmation of truth also fits a prophet's calling. Anna, the prophetess, and Simeon, the prophet, both confirmed Jesus as the Messiah (Luke 2:34–38). Even though multiple prophecies in the Old Testament prophesied of Jesus' birth, the Lord sent prophets to lead the people to His newly born Messiah.

Four tests of a prophet

If false prophets can speak the message right alongside true prophets, then how can we know to whom we should listen? How can we determine who really speaks on God's behalf and who speaks for themselves? The Bible gives us four sure tests of a prophet.

1. The prophet's message must conform to established revelation. "To the law and to the testimony! If they do not speak according to this word, it is because there is no light in them" (Isaiah 8:20, NKJV). To paraphrase, if a prophet is not in complete harmony with God's Word, the Bible, then that prophet is a prophet of evil. If the Holy Spirit moves on a prophet, the prophet's message must agree with the Holy Spirit's previous work recorded in His Word. "Above all, you must understand that no prophecy of Scripture came about by the prophet's own interpretation" (2 Peter 1:20). Since Scripture was given by God, Scripture tests all new revelations. When His word comes today, it will not contradict the truths He has already given. God notes that even if miracles should accompany their message, if it does not conform to previous revelation, we do not accept it (Deuteronomy 13:1–3).

2. The prophet must live a genuine Christian life. "Beware of false prophets, who come to you in sheep's clothing, but inwardly are ravenous wolves. You will know them by their fruits. Grapes are not gathered from thorn bushes nor figs from thistles" (Matthew 7:15, 16). A wolf can be detected by the sheep if they note the way the wolf acts (Matthew 7:17). We can know if the prophet truly speaks for God if they obey His commandments (1 John 2:3). The prophet's character will reflect God's transforming presence.

3. The prophet must confess that Jesus is God come in the flesh. "By this you know the Spirit of God: every spirit that confesses that Jesus Christ has come in the flesh is from God" (1 John 4:2). The statement that "Jesus Christ has come" indicates that the prophet acknowledges that Jesus existed before He became flesh—in other words, that Jesus' nature encompasses both full divinity and full humanity. Jesus did not just appear as flesh; He became flesh.

4. The prophet's message must be valid. "When a prophet speaks in the name of the LORD, if the thing does not come about or come true, that is the thing which the LORD has not spoken. The prophet has spoken it presumptuously; you shall not be afraid of him" (Deuteronomy 18:22). "The prophet who prophesies of peace, when the word of the prophet comes to pass, then that prophet will be known as one whom the LORD has truly sent" (Jeremiah 28:9). Hananiah, the fake prophet, was preaching a pleasant message, but he was not preaching God's message. Jeremiah prophesied of Hananiah's death within the year, and it came to pass (Jeremiah 28:15–17). It makes sense that a prophet's predictions would be reliable if God gave them to him or her.

One caveat exists. God allows for an alternative outcome if the prophecy's conditions change. "At one moment I might speak concerning a nation or concerning a kingdom to uproot, to pull down, or to destroy it; if that nation against which I have spoken turns from its evil, I will relent concerning the calamity I planned to bring on it. Or at another moment I might speak concerning a nation or concerning a kingdom to build up or to plant it; if it does evil in My sight by not obeying My voice, then I will think better of the good with which I had promised to bless it" (Jeremiah 18:7–10).

With this exception, we recognize that Jonah truly functioned as God's prophet, even though the immediate destruction of Nineveh didn't happen. The people's repentance caused God to withdraw the judgment He had intended to deliver. The repentant heart of the people can turn back God's corrective acts. The sin of the people can turn away God's blessing. Jonah records this truth in the repentance of the people of Nineveh (Jonah 3:10).

We need to apply these tests to those speaking for God today, so we can keep from being misled and so we might hear God's leading in our day. I believe the gift of prophecy and leadership functioned in Ellen White, who lived during the nineteenth century. She served individuals, and God used her to lead the development of the Seventh-day Adventist Church.

However, it is clear that "the writings of Ellen White are not a substitute for Scripture. They cannot be placed on the same level. The Holy Scriptures stand alone, the unique standard by which her and all other writings must be judged and to which they must be subject."[1] Her writings uplift Scripture, functioning as a "lesser light" to lead to "the greater light."[2] She lived a God-honoring life of sacrificial service that truly shows the fruit of the spirit resting in her life. She exalted Jesus as fully divine, stating, "In Christ is life, original, unborrowed, underived."[3] Her counsels led a church to success. She had a burden for people, and God called her to minister to them in multiple volumes of writings spanning a wide variety of subjects, from personal religion and health to public evangelism and education, from principles in family and social relationships to the work of printing.

God desires to communicate His will to us today. He uses the gift of prophecy in a variety of ways to lead His people. Prophets function to encourage, to warn, to direct, and to protect God's people. God has said prophecy would exist until all come to unity and maturity in the faith. A prophet only benefits us if we listen to him. This reveals to me a God who seeks relationship by communicating to us—a God beyond my wildest dreams.

---

1. *Seventh-day Adventists Believe* . . . (Silver Spring, MD: General Conference of Seventh-day Adventists, 1988), 227.
2. Ellen G. White, *Selected Messages*, bk. 3 (Hagerstown, MD: Review and Herald®, 2006), 30.
3. Ellen G. White, *The Desire of Ages* (Nampa, ID: Pacific Press®, 2005), 530.

Thoughts to Ponder

1. Have I applied the tests of a prophet to Ellen White? Have I had a negative experience with others misusing Ellen White? Has that shaped my willingness to study her for myself? Do I know the principles of hermeneutics to explore what she says?

_____

_____

_____

2. Would being apathetic toward prophetic counsel be the same as rejecting it? Would it have the same end results for me personally?

_____

_____

_____

3. What role does Ellen White play in my life? When did I last read something she has written?

_____

_____

_____

4. Do I have questions about Ellen White's authority that I need to settle in order to be open to her ministry? Who will I seek out this week to schedule time to talk about her role in the church and in my life?

_____

_____

_____

CHAPTER 13

The King Is Coming

One day Mom left her children at her sister's house for several hours. When she came to pick them up, she thanked her sister profusely and called upstairs, "OK, kids, help put the toys away; it's time to go."

Immediately, three forlorn-looking boys appeared at the top of the stairs. One groaned, "Oh, Mom, do we have to go? We're having fun. We want to stay and play with our cousins."

What Mom thought was a "compassionate rescue" the kids viewed as an "unwanted abduction."

Not everyone views the second coming of Jesus with the same degree of enthusiasm. Some would declare with the boys, "We are having fun here. Do we have to go?" Some prefer the company of their friends to the company of their Father.

Scripture describes two distinct groups at Jesus' coming. One group cries "to the mountains and the rocks, 'Fall on us and hide us from the face of the one who sits on the throne and from the wrath of the Lamb' " (Revelation 6:16, NLT). The other group, responding to the very same event, calls out, "Behold, this is our God for whom we have waited that He might save us. This is the LORD for whom we have waited; let us rejoice and be glad in His salvation" (Isaiah 25:9).

The blessed hope

To be in love with Jesus means that I anticipate His return as my blessed hope. Paul instructs believers to "live sensibly, righteously and godly in the present age, looking for the blessed hope and the appearing of the glory of our great God and Savior, Christ Jesus" (Titus 2:12, 13).

The New Testament alone refers to the Second Coming approximately 380 times. This means one in every twenty-five verses references this important event. Jesus referred to it as a hope to comfort His disciples with the thought that He would not leave them forever. Jesus comes for His children throughout all ages. He is our hope.

"Do not let your heart be troubled; believe in God, believe also in Me. In My Father's house are many dwelling places; if it were not so, I would have told you; for I go to prepare a place for you. If I go and prepare a place for you, I will come again and receive you to Myself, that where I am, there you may be also" (John 14:1–3).

Promise validated by God

Jesus made a promise to His disciples, and later, while under oath at His trial, He testified,

This chapter is based on Seventh-day Adventist fundamental belief no. 25, "The Second Coming of Christ."

99

"Hereafter you will see THE SON OF MAN SITTING AT THE RIGHT HAND OF POWER, AND COMING ON THE CLOUDS OF HEAVEN" (Matthew 26:64).

Jesus appeared to His disciples many times after His resurrection (Acts 1:3). He encouraged them and gave them hope. But this sharing time with His disciples was not the promised Second Coming. When Jesus ascended to heaven, two angels reiterated His promise. "And after He had said these things, He was lifted up while they were looking on, and a cloud received Him out of their sight. And as they were gazing intently into the sky while He was going, behold, two men in white clothing stood beside them. They also said, 'Men of Galilee, why do you stand looking into the sky? This Jesus, who has been taken up from you into heaven, will come in just the same way as you have watched Him go into heaven' " (Acts 1:9–11).

Just as they witnessed Jesus rising to heaven, they will also visibly witness His second coming. He left in a cloud and will come back again in the clouds.

I find it affirming that Luke, a physician, wrote both the Gospel of Luke and the book of Acts. This doctor attests to a flesh-and-blood Jesus (Luke 24:36–43, 50, 51). Luke, who knew about physical anatomy, recorded that this same Jesus will come again (Acts 1:11). How fitting for God to arrange for a physician to describe the return of the resurrected Jesus as a real, physical person.

A tangible, physical coming

A piercing note sounds across the sky like a clarion blast: "For the Lord Himself will descend from heaven with a shout, with the voice of the archangel and with the trumpet of God, and the dead in Christ will rise first" (1 Thessalonians 4:16). This noise literally wakes the dead. Only a handful of Bethlehem's shepherds heard heaven's declaration through the angel choir announcing Jesus' birth. It will not be so with His second coming. Jesus' wake-up call for His children will bring all His true followers to Him.

A glorious flash of lightning against the black sky catches our eye even though our attention is focused elsewhere. In the same way, He parades His coming to receive His children (Matthew 24:27). The whole world will see this victorious moment of God reuniting with His children.

Jesus comes with the combined glory of His father and the angels of heaven. The brightness and magnitude of His glory remains beyond our comprehension. One angel's glory caused trained soldiers to fall back as if dead (Matthew 28:3, 4). Jesus' splendid appearance to Saul blinded him (Acts 9:3–9). Imagine the intensity of the glory when Jesus is joined by all the heavenly angels to come and get us (Luke 9:26; Matthew 25:31). The sky retracts like a roller blind, snapping up into place, and "every mountain and island [will be] moved out of their places" (Revelation 6:14).

He comes with power over death. Believers are transformed as the trumpet sounds. These dead bodies come to life, and the living and the resurrected receive immortality.

Behold, I tell you a mystery; we will not all sleep, but we will all be changed, in a moment, in the twinkling of an eye, at the last trumpet; for the trumpet will sound, and the dead will be raised imperishable, and we will be changed. For this perishable must put on the imperishable, and this mortal must put on immortality. But when this perishable will have put on the imperishable, and this mortal will have put on immortality, then will come about the saying that is written, "DEATH IS SWALLOWED UP IN VICTORY. O DEATH, WHERE IS YOUR VICTORY? O DEATH, WHERE IS YOUR STING?" The sting of death is sin, and the power of sin is the law; but thanks be to God, who gives us the victory through our Lord Jesus Christ (1 Corinthians 15:51–57).

Paul emphasized God's promise: "We will be changed." He had hope in the resurrection and shared it with them. He knew Jesus would come again so that we could be physically together.

Light responds to light. God's people separated by sickness, death, distance, and years come together as one glorious family as the angels gather the risen elect from every direction of the compass (Matthew 24:31). The dead escape from their graves with new, immortal bodies. They rise first, and the rest of the righteous, also having been given immortal bodies, join them.

The timing of God's coming

Immediately after reading about this incredible event, I join with John the revelator, praying, "Even so, come, Lord Jesus" (Revelations 22:20, KJV). While we anticipate this coming, we do not know the "when" of His coming. "But of that day or hour no one knows, not even the angels in heaven, nor the Son, but the Father alone" (Mark 13:32). "For this reason you also must be ready; for the Son of Man is coming at an hour when you do not think He will" (Matthew 24:44).

While we don't know the hour, the signs reveal the nearness of the season of Jesus' return. We need to be in constant readiness for His appearing. Because many are unwilling to know Him, they will be caught off guard at His appearing.

A separation coming

Jesus' coming separates those who allow Him to live in their lives from those who don't. "But when the Son of Man comes in His glory, and all the angels with Him, then He will sit on His glorious throne. All the nations will be gathered before Him; and He will separate them from one another, as the shepherd separates the sheep from the goats; and He will put the sheep on His right, and the goats on the left" (Matthew 25:31–33). God must call out His children. So those who have refused Him will not be given life. This coming really has nothing to do with their judgment. That comes later. He comes for His children. Christ's coming is wonderful for those who have waited for it. But for those who have allowed themselves to cling to darkness, they are destroyed with the sin they have cherished.

You can look forward to it also. Knowing Him, you will be like His disciples, longing for any distance between you to be removed. You will "live holy and godly lives as you look forward to the day of God" (2 Peter 3:11, 12, NIV). Jesus promised, "Behold, I am coming quickly, and My reward is with Me, to render to every man according to what he has done" (Revelation 22:12). Jesus brings Himself as the reward—the God beyond my wildest dreams.

Thoughts to Ponder

1. Would I live differently if I believed Christ will come in the next few months? How would my spiritual life change? How would my passion to share with others increase?

_____

_____

_____

2. Does realizing that this world will not be our final home have an effect on materialism and greed? Would it have an effect on my priorities?

_____

_____

_____

3. How do current events play into the fact that Jesus is coming soon? How do I find the balance between sensationalism, conspiracy theories, and honest recognition of the signs of the times being filled?

_____

_____

_____

4. How am I getting ready for this sure event? Do I deal with the Second Coming from a relational standpoint or from a doctrinal standpoint?

_____

_____

_____

CHAPTER 14

The Fountain of Life

Dismounting from their horses in a garden oasis, they approached the crystal pool with reverence. The conquistador and his men had traversed half of the world to come to the Yucatán land of Boinca to find its hidden treasures. A fountain some thirty feet up the lush green hill fed the pool. As the water jetted from the opening, a fine mist hung in the air, giving the entire area a magical aura. One of the soldiers cupped his hand, dipped it into the pool, and let the water run through his fingers, announcing, "It's so light; like liquid feathers."

Holding his wet hand up so all could see, he said, "It glistens as if I had dipped it into oil, yet it does not feel greasy." Another soldier tried unsuccessfully to float a small piece of lightweight wood and then a dried leaf. Then he said, "This water is so light it will not float an object." A third soldier, cupping his hands and bringing the water to his lips to drink, smiled in satisfaction: "It has a hint of sweetness, like water having flowed through a honeycomb, and smells like a field of violets." With that, the conquistador announced, "Men, we have found it—the fountain of youth!" With that, they all let out a cheer and began to drink and play in the waters.

This story comes from a legend; yet, in reality, men would give their kingdom to discover a fountain of youth. Note I did not say a fountain of existence. I have met many people suffering under the rigors of old age or living a life of abject poverty who anticipated the peace of being laid to rest. People don't want to live forever if it includes degenerating with each passing year and losing quality of life.

The fountain of youth conjures up images of laughing children with boundless energy, playing joyously. It calls to mind young men in their prime with bulging muscles testing their abilities and attempting to impress would-be mates with greater and greater feats of strength. It paints a picture of graceful young ladies whose inner beauty radiates on their countenance. It speaks of the sensations of warm sand between your toes, sweet grape juice trickling down your throat, and the inner raging of the heart at love's first kiss.

In it, I hear the swelling melody of an orchestra pleasing the senses and the sound of the robin song welcoming the spring. It offers the possibility for relationships to grow deeper and relieves the pain and grief of goodbyes for those we cherish. It holds the promise of vitality to go on the next adventure and the fortitude to change your circumstances. We were made to live this sort of life!

This chapter is based on Seventh-day Adventist fundamental belief no. 26, "Death and Resurrection."

The fountain of life exists

I have good news for you—the fountain of life exists! God Himself testifies that everlasting life exists; He freely offers it to us! Once a disillusioned woman sneaked out to the community well to draw water during the hottest part of the day in order to avoid others. She thought relationships would fill her parched soul, but she found her thirst unquenched. (Haven't many of us also drunk from the broken cisterns of Sychar's well and left unsatisfied?)

Jesus asked the woman for a drink, but soon He offered her "living water"—the gift of God (John 4:10). Jesus pointed to the physical water and said, "Everyone who drinks of this water will thirst again" (John 4:13). She already knew that! He continued, "But whoever drinks of the water that I will give him shall never thirst; but the water that I will give him will become in him a well of water springing up to eternal life" (John 4:14). Jesus offers an artesian well of life, a life that flows deep within.

Near the end of His ministry, "Jesus stood and cried out, saying, 'If anyone is thirsty, let him come to Me and drink. He who believes in Me, as the Scripture said, "From his inner-most being will flow rivers of living water." ' But this He spoke of the Spirit, whom those who believed in Him were to receive; for the Spirit was not yet given, because Jesus was not yet glorified" (John 7:37–39). Jesus talks about the Holy Spirit that will connect us to Him and flow from us to others. For all who have been searching for real life, He introduces the Godhead as the life source.

Humans don't go on living without Jesus

Most of the Christian world overtly acknowledges Jesus as the true source of life. However, what many teach about death rejects the truth that Jesus is the eternal source of life. They teach that after the first death many people go on living in hell. How does that work? If sinners did not receive Jesus, how can they have eternal life to live in hell? With this reasoning, either they are eternal beings or God gave them their eternal life—so that they can burn forever.

If we are by nature eternal beings, then God does not give us eternal or everlasting life because we already possess it. "For God so loved the world, that he gave his only begotten Son, that whosoever believeth in him should not perish, but have everlasting life" (John 3:16, KJV). The condition of receiving the gift of everlasting life is believing in Jesus. In truth, those who do not believe, do not accept, do not receive Jesus—His person, His life, His death, His resurrection, His Lordship in their lives—do not have life. "He who does not have the Son of God does not have the life" (1 John 5:12). Sinners do not go on living in some other place, because they do not have eternal life.

God alone has immortality

God's nature and human nature are not the same. By nature, men do not possess immortality: "He who is the blessed and only Sovereign, the King of kings and Lord of lords, *who alone possesses immortality* and dwells in unapproachable light, whom no man has seen or can see" (1 Timothy 6:15, 16; emphasis added). That means that only God possesses an immortal nature. We are mortals—eventually we die.

We have conditional immortality based upon our connection with God. Like a sidecar, we have power for life only as we are connected with the motorcycle. Disconnected, we have no power of our own. All who accept Jesus as Lord of their life receive immortality at His second coming.

The Bible compares death to an unconscious sleep. Jesus described death as a sleep: "He said to them, 'Our friend Lazarus has fallen asleep; but I go, so that I may awaken him out of sleep.' The disciples then said to Him, 'Lord, if he has fallen asleep, he will recover.' Now Jesus had spoken of his death, but they thought that He was speaking of literal sleep. So Jesus then said to them plainly, 'Lazarus is dead'" (John 11:11–14).

The Bible compares death to sleep at least fifty times. This concept of sleeping in the grave does not just pertain to the body but the whole person. "Men and brethren, let me speak freely to you of the patriarch David, that he is both dead and buried, and his tomb is with us to this day. . . . For David did not ascend into the heavens" (Acts 2:29, 34, NKJV). Jesus promises to come back and get His disciples. Why would He make that promise if they immediately went to heaven after death? "Let not your heart be troubled; you believe in God, believe also in Me. In My Father's house are many mansions; if it were not so, I would have told you. I go to prepare a place for you. And if I go and prepare a place for you, I will come again and receive you to Myself; that where I am, there you may be also" (John 14:1–3, NKJV).

Satan's original lie

Satan authored the original lie that humanity would not die when separated from God. "The serpent said to the woman, 'You surely will not die!'" (Genesis 3:4). This was part of his first temptation to Adam and Eve to convince them that they were gods in their own nature. Satan wanted them to believe that they didn't need God for life. This lie emboldened them to defy God and separate themselves from Him, and it is a travesty that the Christian church helps to propagate Satan's lie.

Understanding humanity helps us understand the offer of life. Adam and Eve did not always exist. God does not indicate that Adam and Eve were spirit beings waiting for bodies. "Then the LORD God formed man of dust from the ground, and breathed into his nostrils the breath of life; and man *became* a living being" (Genesis 2:7; emphasis added). Writing it as an equation looks like this: dust + breath of life = a living being; or, as some other versions of the equation state: elements of the earth + spirit = a living soul or person. Humans were not given immortal spirits. Some have taken the term "breath of life," or "spirit," to mean a disembodied entity. The original word *ruach*, from the Hebrew, can be translated "breath" or "spirit," but Scripture clearly states man "*became* a living being," not "*was given* an immortal spirit."

Some have incorrectly used the concepts of mythology and assigned the term *soul* to the breath and made it an immortal entity containing the identity of the person. The Bible, on the other hand, proclaims, "The soul that sinneth, it shall die" (Ezekiel 18:20, KJV). In the Bible, the *soul* refers to the whole person, as is stated in the New American Standard Bible: "The person who sins will die" (Ezekiel 18:20).

We become mortal, living beings at creation

What happens at death to the ingredients God used to form man? If you take wood + nails

= box, what happens when you remove the nails from the wood? Where does the box go? It simply ceases to exist, because the box is a combination of nails and wood. We may remember its characteristics and can form it again, but at this time the box is no more. When the dust and breath of God are separated, man ceases to be a living being. Like ingredients in a recipe, each element is significant but does not contain the end product. Being - dust (or - spirit) = dead (nonexistent) person.

Our thought processes, our memories, our feelings, our awareness, and our ability to reason all are linked to our physical brain. At death, our brain stops working: "For the living know they will die; but the dead do not know anything, nor have they any longer a reward, for their memory is forgotten. Indeed their love, their hate and their zeal have already perished, and they will no longer have a share in all that is done under the sun" (Ecclesiastes 9:5, 6). Another verse confirms, "Whatever your hand finds to do, do it with your might; for there is no work or device or knowledge or wisdom in the grave where you are going" (Ecclesiastes 9:10, NKJV).

We do not go on living in another place after death. We are not roaming the earth in purgatory, nor living in someone else's body, nor suffering in hell. Death simply means not living. To die is to stop living, not a continuation of life in a different state, condition, form, or locale. Sin separates us from God and results in death: "For the wages of sin is death, but the free gift of God is eternal life in Christ Jesus our Lord" (Romans 6:23). Note that death and eternal life stand as opposites. People receive life only through Christ Jesus.

"Our God is a consuming fire" (Hebrews 12:29). He comes as light into darkness and will ultimately destroy the darkness of sin and sinners—who cling to it—in a fire of destruction meant for the devil and his demons (Matthew 25:41). Scripture uses wording such as "destroy" (Psalm 145:20); "will perish" and "vanish" (Psalm 37:20); "devour them" (Psalm 21:9); "become as if they had never existed" (Obadiah 1:16); "whose end is destruction" (Philippians 3:19); "leave them neither root nor branch" (Malachi 4:1); "ashes under the soles of your feet" (Malachi 4:3); and "cease to be forever" (Ezekiel 28:19) to describe the annihilation of unbelievers.

For God to restore paradise, He must do away with Satan, sin, and death. That means destroying sinners. A fire that comes down from God out of heaven will cleanse the whole earth. Then death and hades (the grave) will be cast "into the lake of fire. This is the second death" (Revelation 20:14). "And I heard a loud voice from the throne, saying, 'Behold, the tabernacle of God is among men, and He will dwell among them, and they shall be His people, and God Himself will be among them, and He will wipe away every tear from their eyes; and there will no longer be any death; there will no longer be any mourning, or crying, or pain; the first things have passed away' " (Revelation 21:3, 4).

I see the new earth like a land of endless beauty, like a field of fragrant flowers. Who wouldn't want to live in such a beautiful place? Someone with allergies! A field of flowers causes my body to heave, sneeze, weep, and swell. Consider the wicked as allergic to Jesus' love and righteousness. To them, heaven would be a land of torture.

Jesus provided life so we could live with Him eternally. His promise: "I will come back and take you to be with me that you also may be where I am" (John 14:3, NIV). The God of abundant life is a God beyond my wildest dreams.

Thoughts to Ponder

1. How does focusing on Jesus as the source of life change the way I present to others the concept of the state of the dead? Would it be different if my focus were on what happened to us when we die rather than on who brings us life from the dead?

_____

_____

_____

2. Is the fact that Jesus is the source of life eternal an essential element to correctly understanding the gospel? Does this perspective change how I might feel about presenting it to other Christians?

_____

_____

_____

3. Do I really believe that Jesus' destruction of the wicked is merciful? Why is it true?

_____

_____

_____

4. Jesus wants us to have life eternal with Him. In what areas do I need Him to consume the sin in my life now? Do I feel I am experiencing life more abundantly?

_____

_____

_____

CHAPTER 15

The Custody Battle

All rise, court is in session, the honorable Judge Thomas Benjamins presiding." As the judge sits behind an elevated walnut bench, the bailiff announces, "Please take your seats."

"In the civil case, the plaintiff, Mr. Trueblood, seeks full and exclusive custody of his children. Mr. Steel, the accused usurper, also claims the children. The father charges that Steel, a con man, has kidnapped his children, brainwashed them, turned them against him, and posed as their benefactor."

The real father opens his case declaring his love for his children. He shares intimate details that only the closest of caregivers could know. "Though it has taken me years to find my children, they belong to me. I have been fervently pursuing them even though the defendant has hidden them from me. I know them like I know my own face in the mirror. My son, John, brave as a lion in most circumstances, runs and hides at the sight of a goose. He had a bad experience with one at age three and has been terrified of them ever since. At bedtime I held my Sarah's hand, singing 'Spirit Song' to her until she would fall asleep. Once she was asleep, I would leave the night-light on so she wouldn't be frightened and cry if she woke in the middle of the night. And my little Cheri," the father's voice falters as he chokes back his emotion, "she has always been Daddy's girl." As tears well up in his eyes, he pauses for a moment to gain his composure.

The judge uses the emotional pause to interrupt. Speaking gently yet firmly, he says, "Mr. Trueblood, though I sympathize with your circumstances, this case will not be decided on sentimentality; please present some evidence." And he does exactly that. He lays out the proof—birth certificates, doctor's records, bank statements, school records, pictures with him and his kids, and a parade of witnesses who had also been a part of their lives. Although Mr. Steel claims that Mr. Trueblood had relinquished his rights, the evidence proves overwhelmingly in favor of Mr. Trueblood's claim. The courtroom waits in silence for the judge to rule.

Our view of judgment

To me, this scene of a father fighting for custody of his children best represents the arraignment phase of the judgment—where God fights for our custody. Most often we do not see the judgment scene as a Father working to bring His children home. Instead, we see Him more as a prosecuting attorney trying to convict us in order to dole out a punishment for our crimes. Usually the thought of a last-day judgment brings fear, terror, a sense

This chapter is based on Seventh-day Adventist fundamental beliefs no. 24, "Christ's Ministry in the Heavenly Sanctuary"; and no. 27, "The Millennium and the End of Sin."

of inadequacy, and a view of God that puts Him as our adversary rather than our Savior. Understanding our judgment correctly should produce feelings of warmth, assurance, security, and gratitude, knowing that someone values us enough to fight for us.

Even Christians fear the judgment

We run afraid from the judgment, thinking that God seeks a reason to exclude us from eternity. Many of us secretly tremble at the prospect of God examining our lives, searching for one unconfessed sin or subpar behavior. We picture Him as the doorman at an exclusive club, scrutinizing guests to determine if they fit the elite club's standards. We know we lack completely pure motives. The more we understand Jesus' character and love, the more clearly we recognize that our love still bears the taint of self. The more we comprehend His stature in righteousness, the more dwarfed we feel knowing that we do not measure up. Then we begin to look for a way out of or around the judgment.

"Lying in a hospital bed shortly before his death, W. C. Fields was visited by the actor Thomas Mitchell, a good friend. When Mitchell entered Fields' room, he was shocked to find the irreligious Fields paging through a Bible. . . . 'I didn't know you were religious person, Bill,' the friend questioned, knowing his friend was agnostic. 'I'm not!' Fields said crossly. 'Then what are you doing with that Bible?' W. C. Fields roared, 'I'm looking for loopholes.' "[1] Some of us face the judgment searching for some "loophole" that we might slip through on a legal technicality. Security in facing the judgment comes to us not so much from finding a way to slip through but from finding a new perspective on the whole judgment event.

The multiple facets of the judgment

The biblical concept referred to as judgment encompasses various actions focused on different people, beings, and events. Phases of the judgment apply to the righteous, the wicked, angels, human beings, and God. We often group them all together, creating confusion for what happens and whom each phase targets. Our misunderstanding causes us to fear and drastically affects our view of God and the announcement that His judgment hour has arrived (Revelation 14:7).

For years people have come to mistaken conclusions about the judgment because they combined all aspects of the judgment. In the nineteenth century, a group of Bible students studied about the judgment through Scripture and believed in the imminent coming of Jesus to judge this earth, destroy sin, and take His children home. They preached the judgment-hour message around the world, resulting in the Great Awakening.

In America, those who believed this message were called Millerites, after their founder William Miller. They correctly understood the judgment's timing as October 22, 1844, based on Daniel 7, 8, and 9, and the 2,300 day-year prophecy: "Unto two thousand and three hundred days; then shall the sanctuary be cleansed" (Daniel 8:14, KJV). Starting in 457 B.C. at the decree to restore and rebuild Jerusalem, they discovered that the investigative judgment would begin in 1844. While they worked out the math correctly, they misunderstood what that phase of judgment meant and set themselves up for a great disappointment. Believing the heavens would not need to be made clean, they reasoned that the earth was the sanctuary that needed to be cleansed and believed God would come and destroy the earth and take them to heaven in a single act. Only after the disappointment did they discover that Hebrews explained: "heavenly things themselves" needed to be cleansed with "better sacrifices than these" (Hebrews 9:23).

Having put their lives right with God, they waited for Jesus' coming on October 22, 1844. Their hope sank with the sun as it dipped below the horizon to close the day; their Beloved had not come for them. Would I have anticipated this judgment scene like a child waiting for his daddy to come home with a pocket full of candy, or faced it full of anxiety, like a child whose disobedient actions during the day awaited his father's discipline?

The phases of the judgment

Understanding the phases of the judgment and recognizing what happens in each phase gives us a proper perspective. In the first phase of the judgment, God separates His true followers and claims them as His own.

The arraignment phase, often referred to as the "investigative judgment," serves as a custody case in which God proves His right and fitness as a Father in order to claim His children as legal heirs. Instead of God using the judgment to measure our behavioral perfection, He uses it to present evidence to demonstrate who rightfully belongs to Him. This phase begins before Jesus returns. In order for Him to separate "the sheep from the goats," He places each person in one category or the other. The thought of judgment should devastate those who fall in the "goat" category. But for those who classify as "sheep," this judgment promises infinite rewards.

This phase culminates when Jesus claims His children at His second coming, and together they go to heaven just as He promised: "That where I am, there you may be also" (John 14:3). Because of this, God's children should eagerly anticipate this judgment. Daniel declares that God gives this judgment "in favor of the holy people of the Most High" (Daniel 7:22, NIV).

The judgment encompasses both the righteous dead and living, and in this phase of the judgment, God saves His kids. "So Christ, having been offered once to bear the sins of many, will appear a second time, *not to deal with sin* but to save those who are eagerly waiting for him" (Hebrews 9:28, ESV; emphasis added). God identifies each child who has embraced Him, and they will receive the promised inheritance (1 Peter 4:17).

The heavenly Father, the Ancient of Days, presides over this case and declares that the Son of Man legally possesses the right, through creation and the redemption price paid, to claim earth's inhabitants as His. "And to Him was given dominion, glory and a kingdom, that all the peoples, nations and men of every language might serve Him. His dominion is an everlasting dominion which will not pass away; and His kingdom is one which will not be destroyed" (Daniel 7:14). At the end of the investigative judgment, God comes to get His people and free them from Satan, sin, and death. He resurrects them and gives them transformed bodies. He raises them to join Him in heaven.

The appeals phase follows as the second phase of the judgment, in which every case comes up for review. This phase takes place during the one thousand years, often referred to as the millennium (Revelation 20:5). With all the wicked dead on the earth, and Satan and his followers bound by circumstances and having no one to tempt, the righteous sit in judgment with God (Revelation 20:1–3). God opens His verdicts to the scrutiny of the universe, allowing all to evaluate His justice.

The saints will sit on thrones, and they "will judge the world" (1 Corinthians 6:2; Revelation 20:4). The books of record testify that in every single case God has given everyone abundant opportunity to choose Him.

Questions must be answered for beings throughout the universe. Does Jesus have rightful claim on any of humanity after Adam and Eve sinned? Has God been fair in whom He saved and whom He will ultimately destroy? Did God give everyone an opportunity for salvation? Are any humans safe to save? Who really wants God as their Father, and who honestly seeks only to gain heaven?

This exonerates God's character to humanity, to angels, and to the entire universe. So thoroughly does this vindicate God's name that in the end, "Every knee shall bow to Me, and every tongue shall give praise to God" (Romans 14:11).

The executive phase forms the final phase of judgment. This phase often gets its own billing as the "executive judgment" or "great white throne judgment." It compares to the execution of a sentence in the American judicial system after the appeal process has been exhausted. God comes a third time, and this time He deals with sin. He must eradicate it for His children's eternal happiness. He comes as King of kings and Lord of lords to reign.

He brings His children with Him to the New Jerusalem, setting up the city as His capital upon earth. He lives with us here, on the earth made new. Just as light and darkness cannot coexist because their very nature excludes the other, so righteousness and sin cannot coexist. He must deal with sin.

This final destruction of sin the Bible declares as God's "strange act" (Isaiah 28:21, KJV). God will destroy Satan, death, and sin. "Then I saw a great white throne and Him who sat upon it, from whose presence earth and heaven fled away, and no place was found for them" (Revelation 20:11). No place for them exists because their case shows they reject living under the self-sacrificing principles that govern the new earth.

> And I saw the dead, the great and the small, standing before the throne, and books were opened; and another book was opened, which is the book of life; and the dead were judged from the things which were written in the books, according to their deeds. And the sea gave up the dead which were in it, and death and Hades gave up the dead which were in them; and they were judged, every one of them according to their deeds. Then death and Hades were thrown into the lake of fire. This is the second death, the lake of fire (Revelation 20:12–14).

The issue for all phases of judgment

Our relationship with God serves as the central issue of the judgment. The judgment determines who has accepted Jesus as both Savior and Lord. Not only must we believe He holds the position of God but we must enthrone Him as *our* God. Eternal life comes to those who have fused themselves to God through His Spirit.

The first phase discloses the judgment's true purpose

The remainder of this chapter focuses on the investigative judgment—the arraignment for those who profess that they belong to God.

Together we have celebrated the fact that God pursues judgment as a means to retrieve His missing children. He unashamedly chases after us before the watching universe. A father with a missing daughter frantically passes out homemade flyers to neighbors in a search for her. In the same way, God openly searches for us because He wants us back home where we belong. He boldly declares in Scripture that He longs for us like a daddy watching the horizon for His wandering child. He enlists prophets, like a father might hire a detective, to bring his children back. His unending covenant to us declares that we belong to Him as His children and He delights in being our God.

Yet another claims us as well. This scoundrel has taken advantage of our naïveté and corrupted our innocence. Then, like an angry divorced parent, Satan does everything to prevent us from loving God. He misrepresents God's intentions toward us. He lies about who truly bears the responsibility for our pain. He vilifies the character of God. He cloaks our true identity from us, making us think we were created in his image and not in the image of God. He snatches away any evidence that points to our position and inheritance as sons and daughters. Satan whispers in our ears that whatever family connections we had with God we eternally severed when we bought into his pretense of caring for us and chose to live with him instead of our true Father. He pretends that he is our protector. In an attempt to secure his hold over us, he tells us that hiding from God will keep us safe, hoping to introduce fear of God in our hearts.

The judgment is a custody battle, determining whether we belong to Satan or Jesus.

"Judgment is set and the books are opened" as, before the Ancient of Days and the onlooking universe, the record reveals the truth. Satan, on his side, points to Adam and Eve and cites their Fall as the corporate representatives of humankind. By their giving allegiance to him, he claims legal right to own us.

This accuser of the brothers, who pretended to defend us against what he convinced us was God's tyranny, becomes our prosecuting attorney. He will not hesitate to drag up every evil act of our lives in order to gain a guilty verdict against us and keep us from our heavenly Father. He parades our sinful acts before us, claiming these definitively prove that the same wickedness flows through our veins as his.

Declared safe to save

For us as the accused, it seems futile to even bring up an objection. How can I object when I know that I am guilty of all the charges brought to me? Even as a Christian I have sinned. When I chose God, I put up a restraining order against Satan, and then I proved fickle and surrendered to the devil's enticements. I have both missed the mark accidentally, and I have also, in my momentary lapses of sanity, distrusted God's plan and willfully, knowingly, sinned against Him. Satan's case seems airtight; his argument proves faultless. In the courtroom, my heart cries out, "Who can dispute Satan's claim on my life?"

Then Jesus steps forward to claim me. He spreads His nail-pierced hands wide and proclaims that, though I have sinned, I am joined to Him. His blood paid the full price for my every sin. My record is expunged. As His child, I am "being justified as a gift by His grace through the redemption which is in Christ Jesus; whom God displayed publicly as propitiation in His blood through faith. This was to demonstrate His righteousness, because in the forbearance of God He passed over the sins previously committed; for the demonstration, I say, of His righteousness at the present time, so that He would be just and the justifier of the one who has faith in Jesus" (Romans 3:24–26).

My faith has made me a "new creature" with Jesus living inside (2 Corinthians 5:17). Jesus has fused His heart to mine, and my character mirrors His own. He declares me safe to save. I live in the deliverance from sin that He has provided for me.

This investigative judgment has eternal consequences because God claims those who belong to Him. For God to complete the judgment in full, He must destroy wickedness and the enemy as part of the judgment in favor of His people.

The verdict

We pick up our story where we left off, with Mr. Trueblood waiting to hear the judge's verdict. "Mr. Trueblood, the evidence you have presented to me seems indisputable. I am saddened that your children have been separated from you for this long. Recognizing that they have been with Mr. Steel for this long, I am going to deliver an unusual verdict. I have decided to emancipate the children. They will have the opportunity to choose who they will live with from this date forward."

We have that choice. God seeks after us in this custody case, but the final decision of whom we choose as our custodial parent rests in our hands. God seeks through the judgment to reconcile all of His children who choose Him. The court scene we have sometimes imagined as a criminal case against us, with God serving as the heavenly judge doling out punitive sentences based on the severity of the crime, turns out to be a custody battle with God proving He has the right to claim us. The custody battle ends, declaring the Son of Man as worthy to receive the kingdom, and awards custody of those who have given their lives to Jesus. For those who choose Him, the judgment is good news! The Father, a God beyond my wildest dreams, fights to take me home with Him forever.

---

1. Kathy Bernard, "Reading the Fine Print," *A Catholic View*, accessed August 25, 2016, http://catholicvu.com/Reading%20The%20 Fine%20Print.htm.

Thoughts to Ponder

1. How have I looked on judgment in the past? What fears have I had about the judgment?

_____

_____

_____

2. Does the vision of God fighting a custody battle for His children give me a new view of the judgment? How does it change my feelings?

_____

_____

_____

3. Not everyone will be saved. What part do works play in the judgment?

_____

_____

_____

4. What is the big issue of the judgment? Where am I in surrendering my life to Jesus? Is surrender a onetime decision?

_____

_____

_____

5. How would I share this new perspective of the judgment as good news to others?

_____

_____

_____

CHAPTER 16

Finally Home

I can never go home!" I said to myself, putting reason above the overwhelming emotion that drew me back. Months earlier I had felt just the opposite; I couldn't wait to leave home. I wanted out of the oppressive prison at any cost. With a young man's reckless abandon, I forfeited what I had with my father to gain freedom. To leave, I needed money, so I asked my dad for my portion of the inheritance. Essentially, I stated that I cared nothing about him and wished he were dead so I could have his money. I requested it like a business proposition. He stood visibly stunned but agreed to my demand.

I distanced myself from his emotions, ignoring the pain on his face and his depressed countenance as he handed me the cash from his liquidated assets. With money in hand, I escaped to a faraway country. I partied and indulged every bodily craving, but I could not find a satisfying joy. My fleeting happiness lasted sometimes for only a few hours and other times for mere seconds. Every morning I fought back remorse, regret, shame, and humiliation. I lived for the next lift, like a child going from ride to ride in the amusement park, trying to keep his high. Women, drinking, eating, games, and luxury brought me only momentary pleasures.

Then famine hit the land, resulting in a crashed stock market. It brought me down. I came to the place where I, a Jew, ended up slopping pigs. Picture yourself cleaning and repairing used septic tanks, and you will have an idea of my disgust and shame.

Now as I found myself broke and broken, half-starved and stripped of pride, humbled and humiliated, I ached for what I had walked away from. Yes, I needed someone to take care of me financially, but I needed more than that. I longed for someone who knew me through and through and loved me. Not those who loved my money or attached to me for what I could do for them, but those who loved me for who I am. Why does it take losing something to realize what you had all along?

I repeated to myself one more time out loud, "I can never go home." I had gone too far. The filth of my sin clung to me like the stench of the pigpen, only I feared it could never be washed off. I had separated myself from my father, insulted him before the world. Even if he could forgive me, I could not get close. The community had the right to stone me. Even if they didn't do that, they would certainly shun me for such an insult to my father.

Then the thought hit me: I could go back, not to my home but to my father's estate; not as a son, but as a hired hand. Not looking for mercy, just entering the workforce. I would return like a man off the street. At least I would not starve. So I threw my buckets to the side and began the journey back to my father.

This chapter is based on Seventh-day Adventist fundamental belief no. 28, "The New Earth."

What makes people long for home?

The story of the prodigal son reaches a turning point when he finally hits bottom. Until then he ignores, or masks, the very feelings that might draw him back to his father. Many of us also need something to bring us to the point of longing for home.

A druggie wakes up after his last fix, realizing he sold his mother's heirloom jewelry to get his high. When a police officer arrests a mother for selling her ten-year-old daughter for sexual favors to earn some extra cash, he realizes the law cannot change corrupt hearts and he craves a different world. When an oil tycoon closes a million-dollar deal yet realizes that, though he has it all, he has nothing, he stares out his penthouse window at the setting sun and yearns for something beyond the material treasures of this world.

A jilted lover and an abandoned grandmother, totally different people, both suffer from broken relationships that leave them longing for a better land. A mother slips to the empty bassinet in the room she prepared for a daughter who died in childbirth. For her, this present world without her child will never be enough. A wife sits in her nursing-home chair, alone after her husband of forty-five years has died. This world seems like a lonely place without him; she waits for a world to come.

For me, every time I go to buy a car without being able to call my dad, or have a rough day but know there's no longer a mom to tell my trials to, I crave an earth with death destroyed. When I left my daughter at boarding academy, I cried the entire drive home. I anticipate a land where I never have to say good-bye again.

If God restores what we have lost, such as loved ones and broken relationships, and just takes away sin from this earth—no hurting, no growing old, no disease, no natural calamity, no crime, no broken hearts, no goodbyes, and no death—I would be thrilled to live here forever. God grants these, and this is enough. But God gives to us even more than we have dreamed. God's Word promises a place beyond our comprehension, with golden streets and gates made of pearl, crystal seas, and a rainbow glow from God's throne. Yet these fringe benefits pale in significance to the real treasure of eternity—being face-to-face with Jesus! In order for us to have this life, we must be fused to Jesus now. Eternal life is more than a reward for doing well; it is a result of a living connection with Jesus.

The greatest motivator for wanting a new earth comes in the desire to know our Savior face-to-face. I have tasted His fellowship and reveled in His comfort, but that is not enough. I am tired of talking to Him through the airwaves like a boyfriend maintaining a long-distance relationship over the phone but never having his girl present. I am finished with imagining Him in my mind's eye and giving myself a hug, pretending it's His arms. I want more than the sense that He lives inside me; I want to gaze into His eyes and feel His arm on my shoulder. I need to hear His voice speak my name and tell me to my face, "I am proud of you, Son." I desire His glory to warm my arm as He sits beside me and watch the expression on His face when I tell Him I love Him.

I want to fall on my face before His majesty and worship Him in His magnificence. I also want to hang out with Him in the afternoon and take a walk through His creation, and listen to Him explain the intricacies of His creation. I cannot wait for a new earth. God will remove all distance and barriers between us, and we will finally live face-to-face.

We left the prodigal son on his journey back to his father's estate. While he wanted his home, he thought it was out of reach. But the story tells of a dad who daily watched the horizon for his son and ran the gauntlet past the community who waited to deal harshly with the returning boy. He lost all dignity and humiliated himself to welcome his boy. He embraced his son and welcomed him home.

God the Father longs for this moment, when He can throw a party and be back with His boy forever. Jesus' promise is, "If I go and prepare a place for you, I will come again and receive you to Myself, that where I am, there you may be also" (John 14:3).

Never again will sin raise its ugly head. Satan, his angels, and evil itself have been destroyed. The great controversy has been resolved, and sin ceases to exist. On this new earth, we will breathe righteousness as we breathe air now. He will make everything as He originally designed it. A perfect place: "And there will no longer be any death; there will no longer be any mourning, or crying, or pain" (Revelation 21:4). Peace, joy, laughter, love, and life grow like trees along the riverbank.

"And I heard a loud voice from the throne, saying, 'Behold, the tabernacle of God is among men, and He will dwell among them, and they shall be His people, and God Himself will be among them' " (Revelation 21:3). The God beyond my wildest dreams, love personified, again rules the universe, and earth has become His throne, and we His princes and princesses, sons and daughters.

Thoughts to Ponder

1. Where on earth have I found a place that gave me a little touch of heaven?

_____

_____

_____

2. When have I felt homesick? What makes me long for home on earth? What makes me long for my heavenly home?

_____

_____

_____

3. Where have I gone through separation from loved ones? What feelings come when I think about the possibility of being reunited?

_____

_____

_____

4. Spend some time focusing on God's heart as He longs to unite with His children. What do you think He feels?

_____

_____

_____

5. What concept(s) in this book gave me a fresh perspective on God, His character, and salvation?

_____

_____

_____

Notes

Notes

Notes

Notes

Notes

Notes

Notes

Notes